PRAISE FOR

And the Nobel Prize in Literature goes to . . . *Bob Dylan?*

"Like Bob Dylan, Dimitrios Naskos cares deeply about the most important 'thing made' within—and bequeathed to us by—ancient Greek culture: the *poiēma* or 'song poem.' Like Dylan, Naskos knows that 'poetry and music have been walking hand in hand for centuries.' His 'takes' on Dylan make us feel how taking Dylan's songs into our souls prepares us to face the challenges of modern life."

—**Tom Palaima, Macarthur Fellow, elected member of the American Academy of Arts and Sciences**

"Dimitrios Naskos's new book makes a unique contribution to the existing mile-high stack of Bob books . . . Though the title suggests a focus on Dylan's 2016 Nobel Prize in Literature, the book ambitiously takes on much more, and ultimately serves many functions: biographical, musicological, and philosophical (What is literature?). Additionally, Naskos includes a piece of his own creative writing in the form of a short story based on Dylan's song, 'The Lonesome Death of Hattie Carroll' (a story that preserves the core of the song while simultaneously bringing new life to it) . . .

"Those who wish to explore Dylan's work through the lens of literature will find content on symbolism and surrealism. Others may be interested in Dylan's place in the trajectory of history, science, and music . . . For the uninitiated, early sections of the book work as a primer on Woody Guthrie, the Beats, and gospel music (all key influences on Dylan)."

—**Jon Lasser, PhD, university distinguished and regents' professor, School Psychology Program, Texas State University**

"And the Nobel Prize in Literature goes to . . . Bob Dylan? . . . explains to us why words, lyrics, speech, sounds, and the oral traditions cannot be separated from the 'meant to be read' forms of literature. Bob Dylan is among the most quoted writers in history, and Dimitrios Naskos makes the case for why the Swedish Academy's decision to honor him with the Nobel Prize in Literature was not only sound but also long overdue. A must for every Dylanologist's library."

—**Tony Beram, managing director, Club Placebo and the Placebo Foundation; president, National Association of Ticket Brokers**

"*[And the Nobel Prize in Literature Goes to . . . Bob Dylan?]* is an intriguing critical composition of the life and work of the American troubadour. . . .

"It is a surprising book that transcends time, with a backdrop of soundscapes, traditions, modern movements, and images of twentieth-century American life. The book is a significant contribution . . . to the 'Dylan culture.' . . . This experience is not simply an answer to the question of whether Dylan deserved the Nobel Prize in Literature or not; it is an authentic journey of exploration into Dylan's universe."

—**Professor Stelios Perrakis, Former Vice Rector at Panteion University (Athens, Greece), Former Ambassador of Greece to the Council of Europe**

"Naskos's book . . . has a provoking and well-established multipart aim. It is constructed like a Matryoshka doll. The outside casing is the work of Bob Dylan as a musician and lyricist, which Naskos carefully disassociates from Dylan as a person. The next, more specific casing is Dylan as a Nobelist, and then [the narrative] follows a new and crucial casing: the legitimacy of awarding him this prize for the lyrics of his songs. Can they be considered poetry? Are they literature? Naskos answers the question positively, rejecting the old-fashioned opposition between 'high' and 'low' culture."

—**Alexandros Ph. Lagopoulos, Professor Emeritus, Urban Planning, Aristotle University of Thessaloniki, Greece; Corresponding Member, Academy of Athens**

"Dimitrios P. Naskos asks whether Bob Dylan deserved the Novel Prize for Literature and whether his lyrics can be equated with poetry at the highest level. Billy Collins (former USA poet laureate) agrees; others don't. It is a debate that will never go away. What Naskos reveals is that Bob Dylan's lyrics have 'managed to tap into the world's collective unconscious like no other artist of his generation.' *And the Nobel Prize in Literature Goes to . . . Bob Dylan?* is a brilliant and fascinating analysis of Dylan and his lyrics and songs, making a major contribution to our understanding of Dylan and his work."

—**Andrew Melrose, Emeritus Professor of Writing University of Winchester, UK**

"In *And the Nobel Prize in Literature Goes to . . . Bob Dylan?*, Dimitrios P. Naskos does something delightful and unexpected, approaching the great musician's life through the lens of the question many people asked the day the winners were named. I was one of those people too. This is what makes this book so interesting. It's a charming, readable excursion through one researcher's own journey with words and music."

—**Marshall Moore, Author of** *Love Is a Poisonous Color* **and** *Sunset House*

"Dimitrios P. Naskos gifted us with an ingenious monograph about the life and work of Bob Dylan, as well as his reaction to receiving the Nobel Prize in Literature. Naskos, a musician and writer himself, draws inspiration from Dylan's song 'The Lonesome Death of Hattie Carroll' and writes for us an exceptional narrative of 5,500 words that is incorporated into the book. It's a text that speaks in its own way about racial discrimination in United States, as well as the dark legislation that prevailed at the time when the great troubadour touched upon related issues. Read it carefully, and you will be rewarded!"

—**Triantafyllos H. Kotopoulos, Professor of Creative Writing and Contemporary Greek Literature, University of Western Macedonia**

"Fans of Dylan will be especially drawn to this book, as Naskos is clear about his appreciation for the artist from the very start, even as many at the time of Dylan's Nobel win pondered how a prominent figure in the music industry could be awarded the world's most prestigious literary prize. This book will undoubtedly convince naysayers that Dylan is indeed deserving of the honor."

—Eleni Sakellis, Assistant Executive Editor, *The National Herald*

"In his captivating book, *And the Nobel Prize in Literature Goes to . . . Bob Dylan?*, Dimitrios P. Naskos answers the intriguing question of whether Bob Dylan's lyrics can truly be regarded as literature. Naskos offers a revealing journey into Dylan's life and the influential people and events that have shaped his verses. A word of caution: it's impossible to immerse yourself in these pages without feeling an irresistible urge to soundtrack your reading with Dylan's melodies before reaching the final page."

—Stefanie Naumann, Award-Winning Author of *How Languages Saved Me: A Polish Story of Survival*

"Naskos weaves together the threads of Bob Dylan's fascinating life and iconic work in this captivating compilation. Through a skillful blend of reflection, awe, and Dylan's own words, readers are taken on a journey that vividly portrays the path to his historic Nobel Prize. A well-rounded and engaging story that will leave fans and newcomers alike thoroughly captivated."

—Caroline Walsh, Author of *Fairly Smooth Operator: My Life Occasionally at the Tip of the Spear.*

"An excellent read—especially if you're a huge fan of Dylan's music, as my wife and I are. This author takes you through the history of this great artist's life and career. He will educate you on two major questions that many of us have asked: how does a musician earn a prestigious literature award, and how do Bob Dylan's lyrics qualify him as a superior poetic genius to deserve such an award?"

 —**Nathan Aguinaga, US Army (Ret.), Author**

"For those of us that matured during and after the Vietnam War, Bob Dylan's music turned the world around for us. Even now I remember bits and pieces of Dylan's music that somehow smoothed the feelings we came home with.

"When I first received the draft of *And the Nobel Prize in Literature Goes to . . . Bob Dylan?* it brought back the 'why' of these songs that mobilized the moral compass of people around the world . . . Dimitrios P. Naskos has brought it all back and explained why Dylan was the only artist to receive the Nobel Prize, and it was well deserved.

"Anyone who is a lover of folk music and the biographies of those singers will love how this . . . biography picks you up and doesn't let you down until the stories of his songs and how they came about unfolds. It is . . . a must-read that needs a space in your personal library. It is the definitive work that defines the history of folk music to rock music in the twentieth century."

 —**David "Doc" DeMulle, Editor/Publisher, The Foothills Paper, Inc.**

And the Nobel Prize in Literature goes to . . . Bob Dylan?

by Dimitrios P. Naskos

© Copyright 2024 by Dimitrios P. Naskos

ISBN 979-8-88824-251-3

All rights reserved. No part of this publication may be reproduced, stored in a retrieval system, or transmitted in any form or by any means—electronic, mechanical, photocopy, recording, or any other—except for brief quotations in printed reviews, without the prior written permission of the author.

Song lyrics are not the property of the author. All rights belong to Sony Music. All excerpts and lyrics are cited.

Editing and Translating: Georgios Andritsos
Proofreading: Sofia Verginis, Anastasia Theodorakopoulos

Published by

◄ köehlerbooks™

3705 Shore Drive
Virginia Beach, VA 23455
800-435-4811
www.koehlerbooks.com

And the Nobel Prize in Literature goes to . . . *Bob Dylan?*

Dimitrios P. Naskos

VIRGINIA BEACH
CAPE CHARLES

I dedicate this book
to Megacles Sotiropoulos
and Eleni Naskos,
in memoriam.

CONTENTS

EDITOR'S NOTE 1
INTRODUCTION 5
PROLOGUE 6
PART ONE 11
  1. BOB DYLAN AND HIS WORK 12
  2. BOB DYLAN'S KEY INFLUENCES 29
    Dylan Thomas (1914–1953) 29
    Woody Guthrie (1912–1967) 32
    Traditional and Modern Folk Music 34
    Protest Songs 37
    Gospel 38
    Talking Blues 39
      "Talkin' World War III Blues" (Lyrics) 41
    The Beat Generation 43
  3. COULD YOU PASS ME THE MICROPHONE PLEASE?
    Excerpts from Bob Dylan's Autobiography 47
  4. I IS ANOTHER: BOB DYLAN'S QUOTES 51
  5. THE SUN CONTINUES TO SHINE 54

PART TWO 57
  6. ARE MY SONGS LITERATURE? 58
  7. THE DYLAN ADVENTURE IS COMING TO AN END ... 62
    Nobel Lecture Speech 62
  8. DOES A WRITER OF LYRICS
    DESERVE SUCH A DISTINCTION? 78
  9. A LITTLE MORE DISCUSSION 88
    Birdman (2014): The Unexpected Virtue of Ignorance 92

PART THREE 97
10. I HAVE A DREAM 98
11. THE LONESOME DEATH OF HATTIE CAROLL 102
  "The Lonesome Death of Hattie Caroll" (Lyrics) 102
  The Lonesome Death of Hattie Carroll
  (Short Story by Dimitrios P. Naskos) 104

EPILOGUE 119
  Dionysis Savvopoulos 122

ACKNOWLEDGMENTS 124

BACK PAGES 125
  A SELECTION OF LYRICS 126
    "Masters of War" (Lyrics) 126
    "Only a Pawn in Their Game" (Lyrics) 129
    "Hurricane" (Lyrics) 131
  DISCOGRAPHY 135
  PANORAMIC VIEW: TIMETABLE 137
  A DETAILED TIMELINE
  OF HISTORY, SCIENCE, AND MUSIC (1941–2020) 141

MORE BACK PAGES 165
  SYMBOLISM IN LITERATURE 166
    Arthur Rimbaud (1854–1891) 169
    "Maggie's Farm" (Lyrics) 171
  SURREALISM IN LITERATURE 173
    "Ballad of a Thin Man" (Lyrics) 176
  INTERTEXTUALITY 179
  CARL JUNG 182

SWEDISH ACADEMY 185
  NOBEL PRIZE 186
  A TRADITION THAT BEGINS WITH HOMER 192
    Ezra Pound (1885–1972) 192

The Troubadours of Provence 195
Ancient Greece and Poetry 196
Friedrich Nietzsche (1844–1900) 200
NOBEL PRIZE WINNERS 202
Svetlana Alexievich (1948–) 203
Dario Fo (1926–2016) 204
    Commedia dell'Arte 206
    Metalanguage 208
Rabindranath Tagore (1861–1941) 208
ALL NOBEL PRIZES IN LITERATURE TO 2020 211

EDITOR'S NOTE

BEFORE I DECIDED to edit the Greek version of this book and, a year later, translate it into the American language, I knew next to nothing about Bob Dylan's extraordinary life and work. Over the years, I've occasionally listened to his songs on the radio when going someplace or when the author of this book, a musician himself, has invited me to his place and over a few drinks played some Dylan songs on his guitar. My favorites are "Maggie's Farm," "Subterranean Homesick Blues," "Went to See the Gypsy," "Blowin' in the Wind," and "Forever Young."

A few years back, when Dimitris told me that he was going to write this book and explained to me why he had decided to do so, I encouraged him and promised to help him because I found the concept interesting and unique. And so, after working on it for about two years, Dimitris came over to my place one evening and handed me the printed manuscript. After we'd had a bottle of wine to celebrate the occasion, I saw him off, plopped down in my armchair, and read it in one sitting.

The manuscript is a marriage between academic and creative writing. It is embellished and enriched where it needs to be, and the writer makes sure to shy away from any gibberish, jargon, and pompous language.

Both times I've plunged into this book, I came back to the surface, drew in a couple of deep breaths, and floated on the water, looking at the clear blue sky and feeling wonderful and grateful for being given the opportunity to work on such an enlightening and exceptional project. It is a great journey, not only through the amazing life and prolific work of Bob Dylan but also into the world of music, poetry, literature, politics, discoveries, inventions, and much more that over the years inspired and carved the bard's character.

To be honest with you, I felt a little embarrassed and ashamed for not being more in step with the life and work of such a sensitive and creative singer and songwriter, who has managed over the decades to touch the hearts and souls of millions around the world.

∼

When Odysseus and his shipmates beached their ship on the island of Sicily, near Mount Etna, to rest and search for provisions, their hungry stomachs were drawn by the bleating of a goat. The sound led them to a cave where they found the goat and plenty of cheese and meat to satisfy their hunger. But when the shepherd, a ferocious Cyclops named Polyphemus, stepped in, Odysseus's life and the lives of his shipmates seemed doomed.

"I will eat you last," the Cyclops said to the Homeric hero. But fortunately, he didn't succeed. Using intellect, Odysseus blinded the giant and escaped unharmed.

I believe that we all have such a giant constantly tracing our steps, trying to catch us, imprison us, and then eat us alive.

The life and work of Bob Dylan present an adventurous and captivating journey—one where with his harmonica, his guitar, and his tobacco-rough voice, he began from a very young age to tread a long, rough road that sometimes led to fearsome mountains and other times to pleasant meadows.

Disguised, the giant tried different tricks and gimmicks to drag Dylan out of his path and trap him. On uphill stretches, curves, twists, and turns, hypocrisy and betrayal smiled at him lustfully, and his shortsighted ego gave him a sly wink. Dylan tasted the poison of envy; he experienced greed, and malice made him bitter. But nothing managed to knock him off his tracks. Nothing.

Dylan remains restless and tireless, a dreamy wanderer with a sharpened spirit, with the doors of his soul and heart wide open and his gaze always fixed on the horizon. He is an explorer of human nature who describes to us what he has seen, heard, and felt. Beyond a shadow of a doubt, Bob Dylan is a musical genius, an undeniable titan in the musical world. He is at the crossroads between culture and counterculture.

The purpose of this book is to provide a taste of his life and work that for sixty years has had a great impact on our personal and collective conscious and unconscious minds and the way we perceive and act toward reality.

Thus, let us plunge into his long-standing career and get to know the poet, lyricist, troubadour, and actor Bob Dylan. And perhaps through him and because of him, we'll take a good look at ourselves, understand our true nature, and make an effort to become better human beings.

GEORGIOS ANDRITSOS

INTRODUCTION

LONG AFTER BOB DYLAN was awarded the Nobel Prize in Literature in 2016, I made the decision to enter the labyrinth of his long professional and personal life. Two controversial questions puzzled me. First, did the Swedish Academy make the right decision to award such an honorable distinction to a musician who writes lyrics? And second, do Dylan's lyrics walk hand in hand with superior poetry?

I have emerged from this labyrinth holding the two answers to my questions. These answers come from my exploration of the global artistic, traditional, philosophical, social, and political characteristics of the times surrounding Dylan's birth, coming of age, and adulthood and the acts and events that sculpted and gave color and taste to his character and songs.

The Greek Nobel Prize–winning poet Odysseus Elytis once said: "And poetry is always one, as one is also the sky. The question is, where one sees the sky from? I have seen it from the middle of the sea."

I am sure that millions of people on the planet have beheld the sky through Bob Dylan's lyrical gaze. The work of an artist should make people listen carefully, think hard, and finally, perhaps most importantly of all, be moved.

PROLOGUE

It was a rainy February night in the late 1980s. My primary school has organized the annual Halloween dance party in the famous Lapoze discotheque, located at Ethnikis Antistaseos in Thessaloniki. Being a fanatical reader of Lucky Luke and an admirer of the Dalton brothers, I masqueraded as a prisoner while my classmates masqueraded as pirates, Robin Hoods, Zorros, knights, fairies, princesses, butterflies, and witches.

I can still hear the whistles and the horns. I see the tables crammed with pies, potato chips, orange juice, wafers, and everything else children love to get their hands on. Our parents sat a little ways off in chairs and sofas, talking and keeping a watchful eye over us as my classmates and I got lost in a whirl of colorful banners, confetti, countless balloons, and bubbles, dancing and singing to the rhythm of a popular song.

It wasn't until high school that I was lucky enough to find the lyrics of that song, "Enola Gay," translated by a piano teacher who taught at the music school where I took classical guitar lessons:

"Enola Gay"[1]

You should have stayed at home yesterday
Ah-ha, words can't describe
The feeling and the way you lied

These games you play
They're going to end in more than tears some day

---

[1] McCluskey, Andy, excerpt from the song "Enola Gay," on *Organisation*, Orchestral Manoeuvres in the Dark, Dindisc, 1980.

Ah-ha Enola Gay
It shouldn't ever have to end this way

It's 8:15
And that's the time that it's always been
We got your message on the radio
Conditions normal, and you're coming home

Enola Gay
Is mother proud of little boy today?
Ah-ha this kiss you give
It's never ever gonna to fade away

Right away, I wanted to know what Orchestral Manoeuvres in the Dark's lyrics were trying to express. When I realized that "Enola Gay" refers to the American plane that dropped the atomic bomb on Hiroshima, piling the streets with thousands of dead bodies, the cheerful mood I felt every time I listened to the song turned into grim melancholy. I was left wondering how such a gentle and sweet rhythm could express such a tragic event. And I wondered, *How could I have danced to it so carelessly?*

For me, this hard fact was a true revelation. Songs are not just about the melody and the pleasant or sad mood they can evoke in you. Little by little, I began to understand that singers aim not only to entertain others but also to convey specific messages or certain truths. For listeners to truly perceive the song's substance in its wholeness, they must search for its deeper meaning.

The same thing happened to me in the nineties at a nightclub where we gathered to celebrate the birthday of a friend who was turning eighteen. I heard a Greek song written by Alkis Alkaios and composed by Thanos Mikroutsikos. I sat at the edge of the bar, drinking whiskey and smoking, and observed people happily dancing the zeibekiko as others clapped and tossed red napkins and flowers.

I still remember the impression the lyrics made on my tipsy head, lyrics we all sang along with, elated and ecstatic: "My love made of charcoal and sulphur, how have the times changed so . . . how the need becomes history, how history becomes silence."

Many may know that I'm referring to the song "Rosa," which doesn't speak of some great love as most of us might think but instead is a hymn to Rosa Luxemburg, a revolutionary of the Social Democratic Party of Germany who was arrested, tortured, and executed. Although Mikroutsikos has mentioned this in his interviews, Alkaios hasn't admitted it.

A few years later, at the dawn of the third millennium, the whole planet watched in stunned disbelief as a live broadcast showed two planes crashing into the Twin Towers in New York City. It was September 11, 2001, the same day Bob Dylan released the album "*Love and Theft*," which among other songs contains "Mississippi." In one of the verses he sings, "Sky full of fire, pain pouring down." These prophetic words still make me wonder whether their appearance on this album is pure coincidence or a remarkable insight.

That same afternoon, I found myself walking the alleys of Thessaloniki, shocked by the unbelievable events of the day. Thoughts and questions whirled in my head. After what seemed a long time, I stopped outside an old bookstore in the ancient Roman Agora and walked in to stand over a desk stacked with dusty books. Behind the desk sat an elderly bookseller.

"Do you have books with lyrics translated into Greek by Bob Dylan?" I asked. He stroked his white mustache, studying me with youthful eyes behind the thick lenses of his reading glasses. Then he arose, muttering, climbed up a wooden ladder, and pulled out a book from a shelf.

"Will you buy it?" he asked, looking at me playfully over glasses that had now slid to the tip of his nose.

"Can I take a look first?"

The bookseller contemplated the book, nodded, and handed it to me as if it were made of expensive Bohemian porcelain. As I turned,

I felt his glance follow me until I sat in an armchair among the book stacks and started thumbing through the pages as Chet Baker's gentle trumpet floated from the speakers.

It was on this strange afternoon that I first read the lyrics for Dylan's famous protest songs, songs that rattled my mind, heart, and soul. Right away, I came to understand that the primary purpose of a protest song is to help create a movement for social change and justice for all people on earth, regardless of color and race. A protest song may address the rights of women, ethnic minorities, or homosexuals, or labor rights, equality between people, the antiwar movement, anti-culture, and the sexual revolution. In short, a protest song talks about important issues that shake the foundations of modern society.

I'd heard some of these great songs many times in the past; however, I'd never perceived their deepest meaning—maybe because they were written in a foreign language, or maybe because I'd first heard them before I was concerned with politics and social issues. From that moment on, Bob Dylan began to affect me more than any other artist. As Bruce Springsteen once said: "Bob freed your mind the way Elvis freed your body."[2]

His music and lyrics not only introduced me to unique bands like Pink Floyd, the Beatles, and the Doors but also opened a bright window in my mind to the wonderful world of literature. It brought me closer to the great poems *A Season in Hell* by Arthur Rimbaud, "The Waste Land" by T. S. Eliot, and "Howl" by Allen Ginsberg.

Bob Dylan helped me understand that the song is a many-sided creation where words, sounds, and pieces of eternal tradition coexist harmoniously, conveying messages, dreams, and hopes to the listener.

All the above thoughts provided me with a well-tuned compass in the difficult endeavor of writing a book that tries to balance academic and creative writing to help the reader get to know the exceptional troubadour Bob Dylan and his work in the best possible way.

---

2   https://www.rollingstone.com/music/music-news/bruce-springsteen-elvis-freed-your-body-bob-dylan-freed-your-mind-68215/

PART ONE

"I really was never any more than what I was—a folk musician who gazed into the grey mist with tear-blinded eyes and made up songs that floated in a luminous haze."[3]

BOB DYLAN

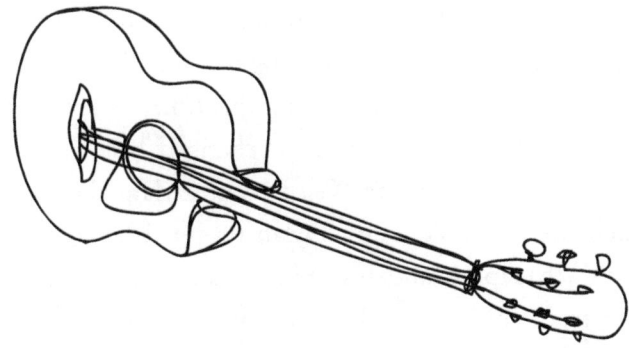

---
3 https://faroutmagazine.co.uk/bob-dylan-death-and-injustice-year/

1

Bob Dylan and His Work

ON MAY 24, 1941, at St. Mary's hospital in the town of Duluth, Minnesota, near the magnificent Lake Superior connecting America with Canada, Robert Allen Zimmerman was born into a Jewish lower-middle-class family.

When Robert turned six years old, his father contracted polio, and the family was forced to return to his mother's hometown, Hibbing. They lived there for the rest of Robert's childhood. With unbending devotion, young Robert listened to blues and country music for hours every day, and when he entered adolescence, he became fascinated by rock and roll.

In high school, he started playing the piano, harmonica, and guitar as an amateur. He also joined a teenage group called Golden Chords. The band played mostly songs by Chuck Berry and Little Richard, cousins to blues, folk, and country music.

In 1959, although he enrolled in university to study literature and the arts, he preferred to hang out at coffee bars, where he listened to and sang folk music. During this time, as several Jews in America have done, Allen Zimmerman changed his name—to Bob Dylan, inspired by his favorite Welsh poet, Dylan Thomas. Fascinated and enchanted by folk songs, Dylan dropped out of the university, and with a backpack and his guitar slung over his shoulder, he hit the streets, hitchhiking to the world mecca of music, New York City.

As soon as he arrived in the metropolis, he decided to visit his idol, the famous troubadour Woody Guthrie, who was suffering from the incurable Huntington's disease, which affects the muscles and leads to the weakening of the body and dementia. Guthrie created the legendary anthem "This Land Is Your Land" about people who fight for freedom and for a better future. At first, the song was called "God Bless America for Me" as an ironic response to the propaganda of "God Bless America." Dylan was lucky enough to play for his idol only five days after arriving in New York.

∼

When he turned twenty, Bob Dylan signed his first contract—with Columbia Records—and released an album with folk arrangements such as "The House of the Rising Sun," along with two of his own compositions, "Talkin' New York" and "Song to Woody," which he dedicated to his mentor. In a 1961 *New York Times* article, journalist Robert Shelton reports, "He was 'a cross between a choir boy and a beatnik,' a 20-year-old with a voice 'anything but pretty.'"[4]

The queen of folk and already famous Joan Baez went on to introduce Dylan to a wider audience. In 1963 he came out with "Blowin' in the Wind," which transformed him into a hero and idol of his generation. The charismatic Dylan managed to touch the spirit and heart of the world and justly win the title of America's most outspoken protester.

Then he wrote "Masters of War," opening a front on all the arrogant bastards who only cared about exploitation and profit. In 1994, fifty years after the fall of the atomic bomb, the song would be played in Hiroshima in front of thousands of excited spectators.

∼

Bob Dylan's soulful "A Hard Rain's A-Gonna Fall," released in 1963, makes you feel as though an enigmatic man has returned from a dark future to tell you what he saw and heard and whom he met.

---

[4] https://www.nytimes.com/2015/09/01/insider/1961-bob-dylan-takes-the-stage.html

"A Hard Rain's A-Gonna Fall"[5]

Oh, where have you been, my blue-eyed son?
And where have you been, my darling young one?
I've stumbled on the side of twelve misty mountains
I've walked, and I crawled on six crooked highways
I've stepped in the middle of seven sad forests
I've been out in front of a dozen dead oceans
I've been ten thousand miles in the mouth of a graveyard
And it's a hard, it's a hard
It's a hard, it's a hard
It's a hard rain's a-gonna fall

On the cover of the incomparable *The Freewheelin' Bob Dylan* from which this song comes, we see Dylan with his hands in the pockets of his blue jeans, walking in the snowy streets of New York City, hand in hand with his love, the artist Susie Rotolo. They became a couple in 1961 and stayed together for three years.

At this stage of his life, Dylan hid behind a veil of mystery, claiming that when he was a child, he ran away from home to work in a circus. This strange and unusual story impressed and interested the public, who wanted to know him better. Later, when *News Weekly* published an article[6] saying that Dylan had grown up in a middle-class Jewish family, he grew irritated and angry.

The Times They Are A-Changing, which came out in 1964, contains folk and protest songs like "The Lonesome Death of Hattie Carroll," which rightly scorches racial discrimination and the dark way the legal system works in America. In the following decades, according to research conducted in the United States, when lawyers and judges made important and difficult decisions, they often drew from lyrics written by Bob Dylan.

---

5   Dylan, Bob, excerpt from the song "A Hard Rain's a-Gonna Fall," on *The Freewheelin' Bob Dylan*, Columbia, 1963.
6   https://www.newsweek.com/bob-dylans-75th-birthday-revisit-our-infamous-1963-profile-462801

Though the public saw him as a guide and a prophet, a peculiar idea lodged in Dylan's mind and began to consume him. He strongly believed that his creativity had hit a dead end. He poured himself into the creation of his next album, *Another Side of Bob Dylan*, which protested social injustice in an indirect and suggestive manner. In this work, we see a different character unfolding.

This new side is clearly demonstrated in the song "Chimes of Freedom," where symbols reminiscent of Rimbaud and Shakespeare appear. Many listeners have connected the concept of the storm with the assassination of John F. Kennedy. The song's symbolism manages to elevate the humble and the ordinary above the world of high thought. Through the lyrics, which are undeniably exceptional poetry, Dylan talks about ordinary, everyday people who, unfortunately, are victims of injustice because they are not rich and powerful.

"Chimes of Freedom"[7]

Far between sundown's finish and midnight's broken toll
We ducked inside a doorway as thunder went crashing
As majestic bells of bolts struck shadows in the sounds
Seeming to be the chimes of freedom flashing

Flashing for the warriors whose strength is not to fight
Flashing for the refugees on the unarmed road of flight
And for each and every underdog soldier in the night
And we gazed upon the chimes of freedom flashing

~

Bringing It All Back Home, released on March 22, 1965, by Columbia Records, was Dylan's fifth studio album. Through the songs, he infused rock and roll with consciousness, soul, and spirituality. Although commercially successful, the album divided his folk

---

7 Dylan, Bob, excerpt from the song "Chimes of Freedom," on *Another Side of Bob Dylan*, Columbia, 1964.

fans, who, seeing their idol experimenting with electric guitars and decibels, became dissatisfied and disappointed. When Dylan made an appearance at the Newport Folk Festival that same year, presenting a more modern and trendy rock style, his die-hard fans accused him of being an ideological sellout, even laughing at him.

Undisturbed, Dylan continued on his course with his gaze fixed on the horizon. In the black-and-white video of "Subterranean Homesick Blues," we see him dressed in a trench coat, standing on the terrace of a building and holding large white cardboard pages with words taken from the lyrics of the song. With swift movements, he throws the pages on the ground in sync with the song. Then the camera cuts to a park on a sunny day and to a back alley in New York City, where Dylan keeps throwing the white pages to the ground as Allen Ginsberg, dressed in a coat and holding a cane, talks with another man.

For this album, Dylan played with the titles of his songs, as in "Love Minus Zero/No Limit," and he avoided using couplets and chorus hooks in the titles as other artists did during that period. The famous "Maggie's Farm" represents America in all its unrestrained capitalism—run not by the landlord but by businessmen, politicians, arms dealers, judges, and the police. When he sings, "I ain't gonna work on Maggie's farm no more," he is saying that he will not succumb to the system he was born into.

In August 1965, Dylan released the crazy and surreal record *Highway 61 Revisited* and achieved one of his greatest commercial successes. The back cover reads, "The songs on this specific record are not so much songs but rather exercises in total breath control."

"Like a Rolling Stone" climbs to the top ten in the USA and at six minutes long breaks the basic rule that a song should not exceed three minutes. The lyrics tell the story of Miss Lonely, a woman who once was rich but now begs among other beggars to get money for her next meal. The message of the song seems to be about compassion and the cruelty of new experiences as old beliefs melt away to reveal a tough reality. It also probably addresses the distortion and contamination of thoughts and moral values in the Western world. "Like a Rolling Stone" is statistically the most acclaimed song of all time and is listed at number one on *Rolling Stone* magazine's 2004 and 2010 "500 Greatest Songs of All Time."

"Like a Rolling Stone"[8]

Once upon a time you dressed so fine
Threw the bums a dime in your prime, didn't you?
People call say 'beware doll, you're bound to fall'
You thought they were all kidding you
You used to laugh about
Everybody that was hanging out
Now you don't talk so loud
Now you don't seem so proud
About having to be scrounging your next meal
How does it feel, how does it feel?
To be without a home
Like a complete unknown, like a rolling stone

In "Tombstone Blues," the versatile Dylan flirts with absolute freedom of expression by saying, "The sun's not yellow, it's chicken," while in the song "Ballad of a Thin Man," he mocks any arrogant journalist who criticized him despite being unable to understand the deeper meaning and essence of Dylan's songs.

With the albums *Bringing It All Back Home*, *Highway 61 Revisited*, and *Blonde on Blonde*, he closed a circle, a trilogy of albums that to many represent the greatest and most prolific period of his career and the best that rock music has to offer. Each of these albums either went gold, platinum, or double platinum.

During that time and in a modest ceremony, Bob Dylan married

---

8   Dylan, Bob, excerpt from the song "Like a Rolling Stone," on *Highway 61 Revisited*, Columbia, 1965.

the model and actress Shirley Marlin Noznisky, known as Sara Lownds, and together they had four children, including Jacob Dylan, who in the late 1980s became famous for writing and singing in the rock band the Wallflowers.

Bob Dylan had great enthusiasm for machines. In his teenage years he rode a Harley 45, and a month after he released the album *Blonde on Blonde* in July 1966, he fell off his beloved Triumph Tiger 100 near his manager's house in Woodstock when the brakes locked up. This is what Dylan said about his crash: "When I had that motorcycle accident . . . I woke up and caught my senses. I realized that I was just workin' for all these leeches. And I didn't want to do that. Plus, I had a family and I just wanted to see my kids."[9]

Rumor had it that the CIA was behind the accident. Whether the accident was deliberate remains a mystery to this day. At any rate, for the next eight years, Dylan vanished from the stage.

It is believed that the artist spent his time in a house in the woods, listening to the sounds of nature and writing songs. And that cannot be far from the truth because, in 1967, he came out with *John Wesley Harding*, which includes the song "All Along the Watchtower," featuring a conversation between a joker and a thief. The song is subject to many interpretations; that is the magic of Dylan. Six months after Dylan's recording, Jimi Hendrix created his own version, played it at a concert, and made it famous. Dylan had made a strong comeback to the warm acoustics of folk music.

Also in 1967, he wrote an experimental collection of poems and prose entitled *Tarantula*, about the turbulence of the times and Dylan's preoccupation with his creative mind. Angry, lively, strange, funny, and brimming with surrealism and modern art, *Tarantula* reveals his humanity and compassion for his country.

Nashville Skyline landed in the record stores in 1969. Dylan worked on it with Johnny Cash, who made music history in 1968 by cutting a live record playing for inmates in Folsom Prison, an

---

9 https://alarm-magazine.com/2013/bob-dylan-triumph-motorcyle/

unsurpassed event even today. In *Nashville Skyline* we hear Dylan sing with a different voice, as though he has clamped a peg on his nose; maybe he wanted to see if we could recognize him.

As the sunset of the 1960s faded away and the dawn of the 1970s rose, Dylan created *Self Portrait* and *New Morning*, two albums that his audience didn't embrace with the same warmth as they did the artist's other albums. Many of his fans felt that the era of the protest song was now in the past.

During that time, in 1971, Dylan made a rare public appearance at George's Harrison concert for Bangladesh in New York's Madison Square Garden. Following major social upheaval in India and Pakistan, Harrison responded to Prime Minister Indira Gandhi's call for international help by organizing this mammoth concert. By his side stood Eric Clapton, Billy Preston, Ringo Starr, Leon Russell, and of course Bob Dylan. The concert for Bangladesh set a precedent for every subsequent charity concert, similar to Live Aid.

In 1973, Dylan initially took on a project to compose the score and songs for *Pat Garrett and Billy the Kid*, a revisionist Western directed by Sam Peckinpah; he ended up making his acting debut by playing Alias, a mysterious cowboy. The story is simple. Pat Garrett, an old friend of Billy the Kid who is now a lawman, is sent to either chase away Billy the Kid from New Mexico or kill him.

Though the *New York Times* claimed that "Bob Dylan's lyrics sound silly and a century out of place,"[10] the soundtrack album was nominated for two BAFTA Awards and a Grammy for Best Original Score. Dylan would play the album's iconic "Knockin' on Heaven's Door"—along with "A Hard Rain Is A-Gonna Fall" and "Forever Young," an anthem dedicated to youth that, according to Allen Ginsberg, should be recited as a psalm by children every morning during prayer at school—in 1997 during a concert honoring Pope John Paul II.

---

10 https://www.nytimes.com/1973/06/17/archives/pat-garrett-and-billy-the-kid-what-you-see-on-screen.html

According to Reuters,[11] Pope Benedict, who at the time of the concert was a cardinal, said in 2007 that Dylan should not have taken part in the concert because he was the wrong kind of prophet and storyteller and had a negative influence on the souls of thousands of young people. I want to mention that Pope Benedict was a music lover who listened to Mozart and Bach, but he didn't like talking to singers. "The liturgy is not a theatrical manuscript, and the altar is not a stage," he liked to tell the priests. "We must not become mere actors in a spectacle."[12]

Nevertheless, in 1997, the flexible Pope John Paul II handled the Dylan case by broadcasting his holy message to the rock and pop entertainment industry: "You say the answer is blowing in the wind, my friend," the pope said. "Not, however, in the wind that blows everything away into nothingness, but in the wind that is the breath and voice of the Spirit, the voice that calls and says, 'Come.'"[13]

The pope continued, "You ask me how many roads a man must walk down before he becomes a man. I answer: there is only one road for man, and it is the road of Jesus Christ, who said, 'I am the way and the life.'"

After a long stage absence, Dylan and the Band plowed through America once again in 1974; the entire tour was recorded on the live album *Before the Flood*. A year later, Dylan returned to Columbia Records and released *Blood on the Tracks*. The lyrics of the wonderful "Tangled Up in Blue" left him unsatisfied, so he often changed the lyrics in his dressing room just before going on stage at concerts. To this day this song is somewhat of a living organism that constantly grows, evolves, and matures.

That summer of 1975, Joan Baez was inspired to write the sensitive and romantic "Diamonds and Rust," in which she revealed details about her love affair with Bob Dylan.

---

11   https://www.reuters.com/article/us-pope-dylan/pope-opposed-bob-dylan-singing-to-john-paul-in-1997-idUSL08626236200703091/
12   https://www.tanea.gr/2007/03/09/world/pseydoprofitis-o-ntilan/
13   https://www.ncregister.com/commentaries/blowin-in-the-wind

"Diamonds and Rust"[14]

Well, I'll be damned
Here comes your ghost again
But that's not unusual
It's just that the moon is full
And you happened to call
And here I sit
Hand on the telephone
Hearing a voice I'd known
A couple of light years ago
Heading straight for a fall

As I remember your eyes
Were bluer than robin's eggs
My poetry was lousy you said
Where are you calling from?
A booth in the Midwest
Ten years ago
I bought you some cufflinks
You brought me something
We both know what memories can bring
They bring diamonds and rust

Around the same time, Dylan released the album *Desire*, containing the hits "Hurricane," "One More Cup of Coffee," and "Sara" (his wife's name). The backup vocals by Emmylou Harris and the wonderful violin of Scarlet Rivera lace the album with special color and sweetness.

With "Hurricane," Dylan returned to protest songs in a forceful way, scorching the unjust imprisonment of boxer Rubin Carter for a crime he never committed. Carter would have likely won the world

---

14 Baez, Joan, excerpt from the song "Diamonds and Rust", on *Diamonds and Rust*, A&M, 1975.

boxing champion title. Despite insufficient evidence, conflicting witness statements, and an all-White jury, Rubin Carter and his friend John Artis were convicted for the murder of two men and a woman in Patterson, New Jersey, in 1966. Small-time criminal Alfred Bello testified that he saw Carter and Artis at the crime scene that night, but in 1974, Bello revealed to the police that he was bribed. "I never saw Rubin Carter in that place,"[15] he said.

A years-long legal battle followed, and Rubin Carter was finally released from prison in 1985. In the film *Hurricane*, directed by the Canadian Norman Jewison and released in 1999, the outstanding actor Denzel Washington portrayed the boxer, and the film became a commercial and artistic success.

The year after releasing *Desire*, together with Neil Young, Van Morrison, Eric Clapton, Joni Mitchell, Dr. John, and Ronnie Hawkins, Dylan joined the Band's "The Last Waltz." For years, the Band accompanied Dylan in his live performances, always in his shadow. I believe the Band combined rock and roll and folk music in a wonderful way and cemented the concept of roots rock. Later, they went their own way until, on Thanksgiving Day, November 25, 1976, after much alcohol, drug abuse, and many hardships, they bid farewell in this historic concert. The 1976 concert ended with all the artists on stage, singing along to Dylan's "I Shall Be Released." The concert was later put on an album and brought to the screen by director Martin Scorsese.

After twelve years of marriage, Dylan divorced Sara Lownds in 1977. That same year, after learning Elvis Presley was dead, he shut himself up in his house for a week, seeing and talking to no one. Later, he told a reporter: "If it wasn't for Elvis and Hank Williams, I wouldn't be doing what I do today."[16]

The following January, Dylan directed and performed in the film

---

15 https://www.mixanitouxronou.gr/o-tifonas-o-boxer-pou-katadikastike-gia-tris-anthropoktonies-emine-adika-20-chronia-sti-filaki-epidi-prokalouse-tin-astinomia-ketous-lefkous-i-istoria-tou-hurricane-pou-egine-tragoudi/
16 https://www.cheatsheet.com/entertainment/bob-dylan-speak-anyone-week-elvis-death.html/

Renaldo and Clara, a project combining footage from concerts, interview clips, and plenty of fiction inspired by his life and his songs. The four hours of material he collected contained many beautiful moments from the tour Rolling Thunder Revue.

Surprisingly, in 1979, Dylan embraced Christianity and released the album *Slow Train Coming*, followed by *Saved* (1980), and *Shot of Love* (1981), all of which contain musical references to religious gospels and spirituals. He won a Grammy for the song "Gotta Serve Somebody."

"Gotta Serve Somebody"[17]

> You may be an ambassador to England or France
> You may like to gamble, you might like to dance
> You may be the heavyweight champion of the world
> You might be a socialite with a long string of pearls
> But you're gonna have to serve somebody, yes indeed
> You're gonna have to serve somebody
> Well, it may be the Devil or it may be the Lord
> But you're gonna have to serve somebody

Dylan's Christian turn led some of his audience to call him conservative, while others found shelter in the church. He had never before devoted three consecutive records to one subject.

∽

In "Dark Eyes," from the 1985 album *Empire Burlesque*, Dylan delivers a first-person narrative about a battered prostitute. In his autobiography, he states: "As I exited the elevator, a call girl was coming toward me in the hallway—pale yellow hair wearing a fox coat—high heeled shoes that could pierce your heart. She had blue circles around her eyes, black eyeliner, dark eyes. She looked like she'd been beaten up and was afraid that she would be beat up again. In her

---

17   Dylan, Bob, excerpt from the song "Gotta Serve Somebody," on *Slow Train Coming*, Columbia, 1979.

hand, crimson purple wine in a glass. 'I'm just dying for a drink,' she said as she passed me in the hall. She had a beautifulness, but not for this kind of world. Poor wretch, doomed to walk this hallway for a thousand years."[18]

In the spirit of the eighties, the music video for "Tight Connection to My Heart" shows Dylan in a shiny leather jacket, dancing clumsily. This new style and appearance didn't suit him at all. Be that as it may, the troubadour continued his work with persistence, dedication, and spirituality.

In 1985, Michael Jackson and Lionel Richie wrote "We Are the World," produced by the legendary Quincy Jones. The profits, about $140 million in today's value, went to countries in Africa suffering from famine. Bob Dylan, Bruce Springsteen, Paul Simon, Ray Charles, Stevie Wonder, Kenny Rogers, Willie Nelson, Billy Joel, Tina Turner, Diana Ross, Cyndi Lauper, and others joined in the performance of the song. As a result, the song became an anthem of understanding, solidarity, and love.

In 1986, Dylan married Carolyn Dennis, an African American musician who had taken over the backup vocals at his concerts. After six years, they divorced in secret, which was revealed in the 2001 book *Down the Highway: The Life of Bob Dylan* by Howard Sounes. The couple had a daughter, Desiree, who looks nothing like him; when she married Kayla Sampson in 2014, Dylan was nowhere in sight.

In 1988, Dylan formed the supergroup the Traveling Wilburys with Tom Petty, George Harrison, Roy Orbison, and Jeff Lynne. The record they produced was playful and commercially successful. Dylan promptly began his Never Ending Tour, which continues to this day and will continue as long as Dylan's persona is still alive.

∼

After years of struggling artistically, Dylan came back strong in the 1990s with *Time Out of Mind* and won another Grammy in

---

18 Bob Dylan *Chronicles*, Volume One, Simon & Schuster, 2004, p 218-219.

1997. Three years later, he wrote "Things Have Changed" for the film *Wonder Boys*, starring Michael Douglas, and went on to win the Oscar for Best Original Score.

"Things Have Changed"[19]

A worried man with a worried mind
No one in front of me and nothing behind
There's a woman on my lap and she's drinking champagne
Got white skin, got assassin's eyes
I'm looking up into the sapphire tinted skies
I'm well dressed, waiting on the last train
Standing on the gallows with my head in a noose
Any minute now I'm expecting all hell to break loose
People are crazy and times are strange
I'm locked in tight, I'm out of range
I used to care, but things have changed

On the same day al-Qaeda terrorists crashed passenger planes into New York's Twin Towers, the Pentagon, and a field in Pennsylvania, the album "*Love and Theft*" hit the shelves. "Mississippi" mentions, "Sky full of fire, pain pouring down," while the song "High Water" seems to forecast floods and disasters suggestive of the raging Hurricane Katrina, which four years later swept the shores of America's Southern states, leaving nothing but rubble.

In a *60 Minutes* interview[20] given in the spring of 2004, journalist Ed Bradley asked Dylan why he was still out there doing tours:

Dylan: "Well, it goes back to the destiny thing. I made a bargain with it, you know, long time ago. And I'm holding up my end . . . to get where I am now."

---

19   Dylan, Bob, excerpt from the song "Things Have Changed," on *Wonder Boys Soundtrack*, Columbia, 2000.
20   https://www.youtube.com/watch?v=hOas0d-fFK8

Bradley: "Should I ask whom you made the bargain with?"
Dylan: "You know, with the chief commander."
Bradley: "On the earth?"
Dylan: "On this earth and in the world we can't see."

I'm sure we all understand who the commander is. I imagine Dylan and the commander meeting secretly on a cold, windy, rainy night in some underground bar with a lot of smoke and dimmed lights. On one side of the table sits Dylan, wearing a leather jacket and a hat, and on the other side, wearing a black trench coat and his hair in a ponytail, sits the commander. I hear them talk in their hoarse voices as they clink glasses filled with whiskey.

The documentary *No Direction Home*, created in 2005 by director Martin Scorsese, shows the life of the great troubadour. At the end of the first part, the late folk musician Dave Van Ronk, wearing a cowboy hat and a plaid shirt, tells us that Dylan, especially in the 1960s, was the voice of America. Through his songs, Dylan managed to capture the pulse of the era on paper, things that the average person felt but could not express. If the collective unconscious by Carl Jung exists, Dave says, "Bobby had somehow tapped into it."

A year later followed *Modern Times*, which includes the song "Workingman's Blues #2," a song that was interpreted in many ways, especially after Lehman Brothers collapsed in 2008. A verse says, "They say low wages are reality if we want to compete abroad."

In the fall of 2007, Todd Haynes directed the movie *I'm Not There*, which tells the life of the bard in an extraordinary and innovative way. Six great actors—Cate Blanchett, Richard Gere, Christian Bale, Marcus Carl Franklin, Ben Whishaw, and the inimitable Joker, Heath Ledger—disguise themselves as Bob Dylan to create a fascinating cinematic experience.

In 2012, President Barack Obama honored Dylan with the Presidential Medal of Freedom, which recognizes people who have made[21] "an especially meritorious contribution to the security or national interests of the United States, world peace, cultural or other significant public or private endeavors."

Four years later, Dylan was awarded the Nobel Prize in Literature at seventy-five years old. The award stirred the art world, engendering plenty of thoughts and comments both positive and negative, especially when Dylan didn't go to Stockholm for the ceremony. (We will talk about all this in another chapter.)

In June 2019, Netflix produced yet another documentary on Bob Dylan directed by Martin Scorsese. These two enormous figures of cinema and music certainly seem to have developed a kinship. *Rolling Thunder Review: A Bob Dylan Story* follows a legendary live tour that took place from 1975 to 1976. The name of the tour was inspired by a hippie spiritual leader who named himself Rolling Thunder and claimed at various times to be either Hopi or Cherokee. Also known as John Pope, for over forty years he devoted himself to medicine and to the education of Indians and non-Indians.

For the tour, Dylan brought together a group of great personalities from the music, literature, and film worlds, including queen of folk Joan Baez; poet and key founder of the Beat generation Allen Ginsberg; Roger McGuinn, a former member of the Byrds; Mick Ronson, the guitarist and partner of David Bowie; actor and screenwriter Sam Shepard; and Joni Mitchell, Arlo Guthrie, and others.

The Rolling Thunder tour wasn't that successful commercially, since the concerts were deliberately held in small venues, but from an artistic point of view, it was exceptional. They all traveled together like a caravan, and the documentary shows rare instances of Dylan acting lively, happy, and outgoing. He would go on stage with his face painted white in an homage to a mime from the French film *Children of Paradise*. When asked why he was wearing makeup, he said, "If someone's wearing a mask, he is gonna tell you the truth."[22]

---

21 https://en.wikipedia.org/wiki/Presidential_Medal_of_Freedom
22 https://www.rollingstone.com/tv-movies/tv-movie-news/rolling-thunder-revue-bob-dylan-story-doc-whats-fake-847231/

In this wonderful documentary that no one should miss, Scorsese brings together old behind-the-scenes images and the present in a way that straddles reality and fiction—fitting for this postmodern world where the boundaries of truth and lies are tangled up and the internet is saturated with misinformation. The beautiful and charming Sharon Stone comes out and talks to the camera, dropping hints that in 1975 she was a groupie of Bob Dylan's. In reality, she was a minor at the time, and the photos of the two artists were photoshopped for the movie.

When the interviewer asks Dylan what he remembers from that legendary tour, he looks at the camera, shakes his head, and says, "Ashes."

～

In March 2020, as most people on the planet were being locked up in their homes because of the ongoing COVID-19 pandemic, Dylan uploaded on the internet a new song, "Murder Most Foul." At almost seventeen minutes, it is the longest song he has ever written, and the main theme is the assassination of John F. Kennedy in 1963 in Dallas. The song is a poetic recitation accompanied by piano, percussion, and cello.

With the streets of New York and Los Angeles reminiscent of a ghost town, at an interviewer's suggestion that we might think of the plague "in biblical terms," Dylan replied, "You mean like some kind of warning sign for people to repent of their wrongdoings? That would imply that the world is in line for some sort of divine punishment. Extreme arrogance can have some disastrous penalties. Maybe we are on the eve of destruction."[23]

Keeping his nose to the grindstone, Dylan released *Rough and Rowdy Ways* in June 2020, his first record with fresh material since 2012. In the song "False Prophet," Dylan sings: "I ain't no false prophet. I just know what I know. I go where only the lonely can go."

---

23   https://variety.com/2020/music/news/bob-dylan-interview-george-floyd-new-york-times-eagles-1234632821/

2

Bob Dylan's Key Influences

BOB DYLAN'S STAR began to shine early in 1960, and right from the beginning, his lyrics triggered a buzz across America. On the strength of that and to understand and appreciate the troubadour better, I want to write a little bit about his main influences.

∼

Dylan Thomas (1914–1953)

Although he lived for only thirty-nine years, Dylan Thomas was widely popular and remained so long after his death in New York City. In his lifetime, he gained a reputation—which he himself encouraged—as a "roistering, drunken, and doomed poet."[24] He achieved great commercial success and has been acknowledged as one of the most important Welsh poets of the twentieth century. His work inspired great musicians such as the Beatles and Bob Dylan.

Thomas was born in Swansea, Wales, and as a child suffered from asthma and bronchitis. His mother took care of him, and his father, a rigorous English teacher, passed on to young Thomas a love for books. Their favorite pastime was to solve newspaper crosswords together in the evenings.

At school Thomas was mischievous, contradicted his teachers, and, save for distinctions in his English class, received low grades. His only and great love was language, and he wrote nonstop beginning in his teenage years. In his writings, one can trace his

---

24 https://lithub.com/roistering-drunken-and-doomed-listen-to-5-famous-welshmen-reciting-dylan-thomas/

obsession and his grasp of the nature of words. He was a terrific wordsmith and injected deep meaning into his poetry. His focus was on the unity and the continuous process of life and death and the new life that links generations. His main influences were James Joyce, D. H. Lawrence, and William York Tindall. Though he was interested in symbolism and surrealism, he refused to follow such creeds in his work.

Thomas did not like to address politics and society's problems. His way of writing leaned toward romance and bringing out an emotional charge. Many critics thus identified him with the Romanticism and modernism movements.

Later in his life, to make ends meet, he worked as a journalist, but the job caused him terrible anxiety, which he alleviated by going to pubs and drinking with friends and women.

In 1933 he completed the poem "And Death Shall Have No Dominion," which immediately became a great success. The poem celebrates the eternal strength of the human spirit through which humanity can claim victory over death. Thomas believed that the dead are never forgotten but rather live on through the beauty of their memory and spirit.

He married the Irish dancer Caitlin McNamara in 1937, and they lived together until his death. Both were addicted to alcohol, and they argued frequently and had affairs with others. But for some reason, they never divorced, and they ended up having three children.

Thomas lived a normal, everyday life. He sat in his office and for hours would write and erase the same poem over and over again until every word left him completely satisfied. Because of his medical conditions, he didn't fight in the Second World War; however, he contributed to his country by writing patriotic scripts for the cinema.

In 1945 he worked at the BBC radio station and gained even greater fame from his poetry. His speech overflowed with eloquence, and his accent was laced with sensual intonation that remains a subject of study to this day.

Five years later, he traveled to America to recite his poetry with huge success. He looked like a rock star, drank too much, slept with any woman he wanted, and enjoyed posing for pictures while smoking. On a rainy night in November 1953, the first twentieth-century rock-and-roll poet collapsed after claiming he had broken his record by drinking more than eighteen double whiskeys in one night. Days later, he took his last breath.

The book *Fatal Neglect: Who Killed Dylan Thomas?*, written by David N. Thomas and published in 2009, draws on startling new evidence, including medical records and a postmortem report, in connection to the poet's death. The book claims that Thomas was admitted to a New York hospital in a coma and died shortly after his thirty-ninth birthday from pneumonia. He had been experiencing issues with his lungs for some time.

Dylan Thomas experimented and invented new techniques in literary language. Poet and professor of philology Kimon Friar eloquently explains, "Thomas recovered the word from the decay of the everyday friction and placed it on a symbolic conceptual level that extends to metaphysical vision. Thomas is playing with the words. He merges the colloquial with the archaic and instills idioms and slang. The alternating images, the long paragraphs that run through the poems in one breath, the peculiar use of syntax, the wealth of associations, the invention, the puns, and the musical flow of his expression, bear witness to a poet in search of a range of emotions and metaphysical meanings."[25]

Today Thomas is one of the most prominent figures of modern prose and poetry. His most famous poem is "Do not go gentle into that good night."[26]

> Do not go gentle into that good night,
> Old age should burn and rave at close of day;

---

25 https://www.booksite.gr/ntulan-tomas.html
26 Thomas, Dylan, 'Do not go gentle into that good night', on *Collected Poems* 1934-1952, Dent, 1952.

Rage, rage against the dying of the light.

Though wise men at their end know dark is right,
Because their words had forked no lightning they
Do not go gentle into that good night.

Good men, the last wave by, crying how bright
Their frail deeds might have danced in a green bay,
Rage, rage against the dying of the light.

Wild men who caught and sang the sun in flight,
And learn, too late, they grieved it on its way,
Do not go gentle into that good night.

Grave men, near death, who see with blinding sight
Blind eyes could blaze like meteors and be gay,
Rage, rage against the dying of the light.

And you, my father, there on the sad height,
Curse, bless, me now with your fierce tears, I pray.
Do not go gentle into that good night.
Rage, rage against the dying of the light.

I believe this poem means that life should not be easily surrendered, no matter how full that life has been. The speaker emphasizes that one should fight fiercely and strongly against death.

Woody Guthrie (1912–1967)

American songwriter, author, and folk icon Woody Guthrie was considered the artist who most profoundly influenced Bob Dylan. His song "This Land Is Your Land" became an alternative national anthem that inspired and stirred up social movements. Woody was constantly creative, covering political, social, historical, philosophical, and romantic themes. At his concerts, he went on stage with these words on his guitar: THIS MACHINE KILLS FASCISTS.

In 1947, Woody completed the writing of his only fully realized novel, *House of Earth*. But he did not publish it. After many years, the book fell into the hands of the historian Douglas Brinkley, and in collaboration with the actor Johnny Depp, they published and promoted it successfully.

The back cover reads: "House of Earth is Woody Guthrie's only fully realized novel—a powerful portrait of Dust Bowl America, filled with the homespun lyricism and authenticity that have made his songs a part of our national consciousness."[27] The novel is a sad portrait of hardship and hope set against a brutal landscape. The story takes place in the 1930s, a period full of dust storms that destroyed fields and crops all the way to the Canadian border. An ordinary couple dreams about a better life and searches for meaning and love in a corrupt world. The book bears similarities to the masterpiece *The Grapes of Wrath* by John Steinbeck and shows us that the soil we step on, the water we drink, and the air we breathe are universal properties and should belong to us all.

Generously and uncompromisingly, Woody Guthrie gave us a powerful story of America. The legacy that this daring and clever artist passed on to us is the unshakable realization that a guitar, a song, and an honest book can become weapons against inhumane political parties and powerful lobbies.

As you can see, Dylan Thomas, the first unbending rock-and-roll poet, and Woody Guthrie, who wrote about ecumenical issues promoting understanding, solidarity, and love without racial divisions, are the two main wellsprings of Bob Dylan's inexhaustible and unwavering creative path.

∼

---

27 https://www.goodreads.com/book/show/15819071-house-of-earth

Traditional and Modern Folk Music

Modern folk music was born in the Western world in 1950. It stemmed from a folk tradition arising alongside the labor movement instigated at the beginning of the twentieth century. This modern folk period reached its peak in the 1960s and remained centered in America.

Umberto Fiori—poet, lyricist, and singer of the rock band Stormy Six—states in his book *Joe Hill, Woody Guthrie, Bob Dylan: A History of Popular Songs in the USA*: "Everything begins to gain popular appeal through Joe Hill, whose life as a worker, trade unionist, and songwriter and above all the method of his death—executed on false charges of murder, through a bogus trial—has since inspired countless artists, from Woody Guthrie and Pete Seeger to Bob Dylan, Phil Ochs and Joan Baez."[28]

Joe Hill (1879–1915) was not only a singer of traditional folk music but also a new form of proletarian artist. Joe was interested in creating an entire labor movement whose sole purpose was propaganda. He strongly believed that songs should not just be entertaining and exciting; they ought to take a stance on universal issues that concern people every day.

The three major personalities that influenced the new 1960s folk were Woody Guthrie, Pete Seeger, and Jack Elliott. The last two, though they wrote quite important songs, are specifically lauded as performers who through the oral tradition preserved a melodic richness that established a ready-made repertoire for new lyricists.

There were many other significant figures of the folk movement. Harry Smith (1923–1991) was an American polymath who realized the value of prewar recordings. His musical anthologies were infused with social content, which he supplemented with smart and intelligent commentary.

At this point, we cannot omit another great figure of folk music, jazz, and blues: Dave Van Ronk (1936–2002). Dave was a friend of

---

28 https://www.lifo.gr/culture/music/folk-stin-ameriki-apo-ton-fonta-troysa

Bob Dylan, but also in a way his mentor. Nicknamed "the Mayor of MacDougal Street" due to his vast knowledge of jazz and blues, Dave was a formidable performer for four decades and in 1996 received a Grammy for the traditional folk song "Another Time and Place."

Upon Dylan's first arrival in New York, Dave put him up in his Greenwich Village apartment, where they smoked, drank, and listened to old songs for hours on end. Dave initiated Dylan into the magical, poetic world of Gérard de Nerval, Guillaume Apollinaire, and Rimbaud.

The two men once had an argument about the well-known traditional song "The House of the Rising Sun." Dave arranged it, and without asking for his permission, Dylan included it on his debut album. The long and short of it was that Dylan decided to add Dave's name to the album, and thus the misunderstanding was peacefully resolved. Later, on the back cover of one of his albums, Dave included a message: "Let's say it, so I'm done with it. Apparently, I learned a lot more from Dylan than he learned from me."[29] Dylan, in his book *Chronicles*, answers: "Dave came from the land of giants. He'd towered over the street like a mountain but would never break into the big time. It just wasn't where he pictured himself."[30] The two artists maintained a sporadic but warm relationship and appeared together at a concert to support political Chilean prisoners in 1974.

Having gained quite a good reputation, Bob Dylan traveled to England in May 1964. There, he listened to the Beatles, the Rolling Stones, and the Animals, bands that created a completely different sound for the audience. When he returned to New York after his concert at London's Royal Albert Hall, Dylan said, "God, you've got to hear what's going on over there. Eric Burdon and do you know the Animals? They turned 'The House of the Rising Sun' into a rock song. Rock! It's fuckin' wild. It blew my mind."[31]

Many believe that the Animals gave impetus to the new genre

---

29 https://www.lifo.gr/culture/music/folk-stin-ameriki-apo-ton-fonta-troysa
30 https://www.robertchristgau.com/xg/rock/dylan-05.php
31 https://www.lifo.gr/culture/music/folk-stin-ameriki-apo-ton-fonta-troysa

coined "folk rock." The shock Dylan received was so powerful that from that moment, he decided to move away from protest folk songs and write his own lyrics, telling the songwriter Phil Ochs (1940–1976), "The stuff you're writing is bullshit because politics is bullshit. It's all unreal. The only thing that's real is inside you. Your feelings. Just look at the world you're writing about, and you'll see you're wasting your time. The world is, well . . . it's just absurd."[32]

I have the impression that Dylan exaggerated with the above statement, because Ochs was a wonderful artist who knew very well what he was protesting about, and he paid the price for his passion with his own life (he hung himself in his sister's house after years of drinking and paranoid tendencies). Ochs managed to instill his wits, sardonic humor, and deep humanism and political activism in his clairvoyant lyrics. He wrote numerous songs and released six records in the 1960s.

Dylan realized that folk was evolving at a rapid pace and that if he wanted to stay in the spotlight, he should turn his attention to electric guitars and higher decibels.

To return to the subject of the rise of modern folk, when the Second World War came to an end, American families—justifiably yearning for social safety and security after the terrifying experience of war and wanting a peaceful and beautiful life spent enjoying the material goods now pouring into the market—decided to move from the cities to the newly built houses in the suburbs. A confrontation between capitalism and communism flared up in the 1950s, and a rowdy teenage ethos erupted. These sexually liberated rioters seemed capable of uprooting the deeply rooted conservatism and traditions of past generations. The religious, proud patriots of the older generation held fast to tenets of honor, virtue, marriage, and generally a life and way of behaving that seemed obsolete to their children.

Contrasted with rock and roll, which has more to do with dancing and diffusing the tension of the body than anything else, modern folk

---

32   https://www.rollingstone.com/music/music-news/bob-dylan-an-intimate-biography-part-two-237760/

of the 1960s was part of a spiritual revolution. By promoting a more humane working environment, this genre connected with a leftist ideology and the civil rights and labor movements.

Countless teenagers hungry for a new way of life needed idols who could free their minds, spirits, and emotions. Songwriters whose music was banned, such as Woody Guthrie, became voices for these teenagers' reactions. Modern folk music merged the traditional music of America with the concerns of students and everyday people and encouraged the masses to create their own reality.

Authentic modern folk music had absolutely nothing to do with the conventions of the entertainment industry. The performer played a crucial role; without his authenticity and strong personality, the communication of strong messages would have been impossible. And the people warmly embraced the messages because they coexisted harmoniously with the melodies.

When Woody Guthrie's health began to deteriorate in the early 1960s, Bob Dylan took over as his successor, becoming the steadfast hero of an entire generation. Along with Joan Baez, he expressed his opposition to racism and supported the civil rights movement. They both protested against the unfair treatment of African Americans and fought for the elimination of social discrimination.

Protest Songs

In the 1960s, social movements called for the abolition of harsh measures imposed by governments. People supported women's suffrage, the sexual revolution, labor and human rights, and the fairest treatment of problems that troubled citizens. Many amassed against war and animal abuse, and later on, people took a strong stance in favor of protecting the environment.

Protest songs comprise a type of music that highlights a social issue or political situation like those listed above. The lyrics are often associated with antiauthoritarian movements that desire immediate change of regimes, while their musical character stems from the folk traditions of the place. A protest song is not always straightforward and accusatory; it can indirectly and obliquely pass on the desired message. For example, Lead Belly's "Goodnight, Irene," although it seemingly refers to love, is thematically about the marginalization and exclusion of people in society.

Sociologist R. Serge Denisoff[33] tells us that protest songs are used by leftist governments for propaganda and persuasion. He also claims that this kind of song is rooted in the religious hymns and psalms of Protestant revolutionary movements. Denisoff divides the genre into two categories: "magnetic" songs attract believers, and "rhetorical" songs express indignation.

Several scholars consider the melodies of protest songs to be less significant than their lyrics. Other scholars believe that protest songs become more effective if they contain melodies with references to cultural traditions. Whatever the truth is, the protest song plays an important and defining role in any generation that rises, resists, and succeeds through endless struggles in changing the world.

The poem "Ode to Joy" by Friedrich Schiller and set to music by Beethoven, though it belongs to another century and is not related to protest songs, could be seen as an indirect protest, just like Lead Belly's "Goodnight, Irene." This poem expresses solidarity, love, and beauty and encourages all people to stay united in the world, free from wars and conflicts.

∼

Gospel

Gospel is the Old English translation of a latinized Greek phrase meaning "good news": ευαγγέλιον, ευ "good" + άγγελος "messenger." Today gospel as it relates to music refers to a genre of

---
33   https://en.wikipedia.org/wiki/Protest_song

African American music born in the Protestant church of America, incorporating elements of spirituals and blues.

From the early eighteenth to the nineteenth century, the millions of African slaves arriving by force and brutal violence in Brazil and America carried in their souls rhythms from their homeland. Over the years, under adverse conditions, they clothed these rhythms with melodies of the Christian tradition.

The main subject matter of gospel lyrics is the sorrow and anger of enslaved people. Since they were not allowed any other means of entertainment, they often sang while working the fields. Through the melodies, they prayed for their wounds to heal and their tribulations to end.

Martin Luther's hymns were the first to be assimilated by African Americans. Overflowing with faith and hope, they sang in the churches—either a cappella or with musical accompaniment—texts taken mainly from the Old Testament. Religious music was their way out and their redemption; enslaved people saw a similarity between their own oppression and the oppression suffered by the Jews of the Bible.

When Dylan converted to Christianity in the late 1970s, he created records based aesthetically on gospel and spirituals. As I mentioned earlier, we can hear these influences on the albums *Slow Train Coming*, *Saved*, and *Shot of Love*.

∾

Talking Blues

This unpredictable troubadour also engaged seriously with the blues. In fact, Bob Dylan created a famous song in the "talking blues" tradition.

On a cold and rainy night in 1963, Dylan wrote "Talkin' World War III Blues," which narrates a dream about World War III. This thought triggered concern in Americans during the Cold War. The year before, the dramatic Cuban missile crisis had seized the world's attention. For thirteen days, people anxiously listened and read about the developing crisis, worrying that our beautiful planet was a volcano about to erupt.

After endless hours of negotiation, President Kennedy and Premier Nikita Khrushchev put an end to the geopolitical calamity. Khrushchev agreed to remove the missiles from Cuba, and Kennedy agreed to respect the territorial integrity and sovereignty of the island.

Talking blues is a form of folk and country music characterized by speech with free melody but strict rhythm. Christopher Allen Bouchillon of Oconee County, South Carolina, known as "the Comedian of the South," is credited with the name of this musical genre since he was the first to record a song of this narrative form, at Columbia Records in Atlanta in 1926. One year later, and in a similar style, he completed "Born in Hard Luck."

In talking blues, you hear a flat voice that is very close to the tone of normal speech or poetry recitation. At the end of each stanza, consisting of two pairs of verses that rhyme, the singer continues to speak, adding a fifth verse in an undefined metric.

In the beginning, the theme was often related to popular humor. Typical examples are Woody Guthrie's "Mean Talkin' Blues" and "Talkin' Hard Work," songs he dedicated to Christopher Allen Bouchillon. In the following decades, the genre morphed, and talking blues began to include protest songs, lending particular gravity to the political and social content of the lyrics, such as in *Talking Union and Other Union Songs*, an album with Pete Seeger, Lee Hays, and Millard Lampell. When Johnny Cash wanted to write a song recounting his trip to Vietnam with his wife, June Carter Cash, he chose the form of talking blues to express his opposition to the war.

According to music historian Manfred Helfert,[34] musician and writer John Greenway's 1958 album *Talkin' Blues*, featuring songs by Woody Guthrie and Tom Glaser, was an inexhaustible source of inspiration for Bob Dylan.

---

34 https://en.wikipedia.org/wiki/Talking_blues

"Talkin' World War III Blues" (Lyrics)[35]

One time ago crazy dream came to me
I dreamt I was walkin' into World War Three
Went to the doctor the very next day
To see what kinda words he could say
Said, "It was a bad dream
I wouldn't worry about it none, though
They were my own dreams, were only in your head"

I said, "Hold it, Doc, a World War passed through my brain"
He said, "Nurse, get your pad, the boy's insane"
He grabbed my arm, I said, "Ouch!"
As I landed on the psychiatric couch
Said, "Tell me about it"

Well, the whole thing started at three o'clock fast
It was all over by quarter past
I was down in the sewer with some little lover
When I peeked out from a manhole cover
Wondering who turned the lights on us

Well, I got up and I walked around
Up and down the lonesome town
I stood on, wondering which way to go
I lit a cigarette on a parking meter
And walked on down the road
It was a normal day

Well, I rung me fallout shelter bell
And I leaned my head, and I gave a yell
"Give me a string bean, I'm a hungry man"
Shotgun fired and away I ran

---

35 Dylan, Bob, Talkin' World War III Blues, on *The Freewheelin' Bob Dylan*, Columbia, 1963.

I don't blame them too much though, I know I looked funny

Down the corner by the hot dog stand
I seen a man
I said, "Howdy, friend, I guess there's just us two"
He screamed a bit and away he flew
Thought I was a Communist

Well, I spied me a girl before she could leave
I said, "Let's go play Adam and Eve"
I took her by the hand and my heart was thumpin'
When she said, "Hey, man, you crazy or something?
You seen what happened last time they started"

Well, I seen me a Cadillac window uptown
There was nobody around
I got into the driver's seat and I drove down 42nd street
In my Cadillac
Good car to drive after a war

Well, I remember seein' some ad
So I turned on my Conelrad,
But I didn't pay the Con Ed bill
So the radio didn't work so well,
Turned on my record player
It was Rock-A-Day Johnny singin', "Tell your ma, tell your pa
Our loves are gonna grow ooh wah, ooh wah"

I was feelin' kinda lonesome and blue,
I needed somebody to talk to
So I called up the operator of time,
Just to hear a voice of some kind
"When you hear the beep, it will be three o'clock"
She said that for over an hour and I hung up

Well, the doctor interrupted me just about then
Sayin', "Hey, I've been havin' the same old dreams
But mine was a little different, you see
I dreamt the only person left after the war was me
I didn't see you around"

Well, now time passed and now it seems
Everybody's having them dreams
Everybody sees their self walkin' around with no one else
Half the people can be part right all of the time and
Some of the people can be all right part of the time but
All the people can't be all alright all of the time
I think Abraham Lincoln said that
"I'll let you be in my dreams if I can be in yours"
I said that

~

The Beat Generation

Born in America after the Second World War, during the Cold War era, this avant-garde literary movement stood in opposition to consumerism, which was overwhelming. While the media promoted the model of a better and more comfortable life, the concerns of culture, art, and politics were sidelined. Beat writers declared their contempt for the vulgarity of capitalism and the industrialization of cities. They opposed the lifestyle of a society that considered intellectual and emotional diversity a crime.

Among the three most distinguished figures of the Beat generation was Jack Kerouac, who wrote *On the Road*. Though it is infused with a sense of loss and sadness, the story tells us that life is full of choices that determine our fate. Kerouac suggests a return to a more meaningful and authentic life. This idea sent a million young people out on the street wearing blue jeans and white T-shirts.

Allen Ginsberg was another singular figure of the movement.

Through his famous poem "Howl," a mad celebration of nonconformity, he asked people to turn their backs on capitalism, exploitation, repression, and subjugation.

The third noteworthy Beat writer, William Burroughs, wrote one of the most chaotic novels ever written, *Naked Lunch*. Using the writing technique of Dadaism (for the Beats, the word "Dada" meant everything and nothing), Burroughs presents his apocalyptic vision of the world along with his drug addiction.

The Beat writers were intellectuals and artists who lived life to the fullest and against the norms of society. Because of their attitude toward freedom of expression and conventional academic traditions, they were considered bohemians and outsiders. Without a manifesto to guide them, these writers lived in a constant search for new experiences and wrote without misgivings.

The word "beat" was first used by bebop musicians (a type of jazz that relies more on dissonance and reaction). In underworld slang, the word often means "defeated" or "poor." But Kerouac gave a more spiritual meaning to the concept by speaking of "beatitude," meaning bliss—bliss and an awakening through the constant study of books and intensely personal experiences. Over the years, the Beat writers came to discover new ways of writing; they sought absolute truth and embraced the philosophy of Zen Buddhism. They continued to rebel, always dreaming of a better world.

As time rolled by, they integrated the culture of African Americans and bebop music. Within their poetic and literary circles, you could meet Charlie Parker, Dizzy Gillespie, Thelonious Monk, Miles Davis, and Charles Mingus. These legends of jazz inspired the Beats with their rhythm and improvisations.

Artistically, the Beats identified with the Romantic ideology of William Blake, Percy Bysshe Shelley, Walt Whitman, and D. H. Lawrence (though he was a modernist), as well as with the Romantic components of American transcendentalism and the civil disobedience of Henry David Thoreau. They particularly admired William

Blake (1757–1827), who stood against classicism, the Enlightenment, the society of the time, and the hypocrisy that suffocated it. In the poem "The Song of Liberty," William Blake tells us that every living thing is sacred; he celebrates creative intelligence and criticizes forces that prevent imagination, expression, and the creative potential of humans from coming to full bloom. For this reason, he calls us to fight for our freedom.

The Beat writers, like the Romantics, loved nature, but they were also influenced by the attitude of displaced and insane people who saw society as absurdly square, rejecting its discipline and its codes. The Beats' anarchist, antifascist, and antiracist way of thinking influenced younger generations of artists, such as Patti Smith and Bob Dylan.

Jack Kerouac coined the term "Beat generation." In society, this term denoted a vague but battered psychological state, while its spiritual state was associated with nobility, innocence, blessedness, and the pursuit of a more visionary consciousness that man alone could create through music, meditation, drugs, mantras, and poetry.

To Kerouac, spontaneous writing was similar to jazz improvisation. The liberated movements of jazz players and logical thinking were incompatible. The best writing and the best solo jazz performances took place without the artist thinking about his work.

The Beats called into question not only the modernism of Ezra Pound, T. S. Eliot, William Faulkner, Thomas Wolfe, and Henry Miller but also the surrealism of Guillaume Apollinaire, Paul Éluard, Pierre Reverdy, and Federico García Lorca. Finally, the Beats criticized the existentialism of Luis-Ferdinand Céline, Jean-Paul Sartre, and Albert Camus.

What disturbed literary critics the most was the Beats' penchant for negativity. They believed that the Beats' way of life was at war with everything President Eisenhower stood for: Mom, Dad, marriage, savings, organized religion, literary elegance, regulations, costumes, and higher education. The Beat generation was a movement of enlightened, demented, unconventional, and marginalized young people who were either disillusioned or defeated by the system. They realized that they did not fit into the uniform of a loyal soldier nor in the tailored suit of a businessman.

The Beat writers were baptized beatniks by journalist Herb Caen. The term might be a portmanteau of "Beat" and the Russian Sputnik satellite. Kerouac considered such a term derogatory. Caen went on to ridicule their literary movement in the *San Francisco Chronicle*,[36] claiming their followers embraced decadent communist ideals without realizing that the world was modernizing and evolving and going in a completely different direction. Since then, the term "beatnik" has been associated with revolutionaries, antiauthoritarians, and anarchists.

To summarize, the Beat generation deeply influenced the art of the twentieth century in all its forms. Beat poetry and prose is still taught in many universities around the world. It also influenced rock music and groups like the Beatles, Pink Floyd, and the Doors. Many important artists kept in touch with the Beat writers, especially Bob Dylan, who maintained close relations with Allen Ginsberg.

---

36 https://www.sfgate.com/entertainment/article/how-herb-caen-named-a-generation-3018725.php

3

Could You Pass Me the Microphone Please?
Excerpts from Bob Dylan's Autobiography[37]

WHAT REALLY SET me apart in these days was my repertoire. It was more formidable than the rest of the coffeehouse players, my template being hard-core folk songs backed by incessantly loud strumming. I'd either drive people away or they'd come in closer to see what it was all about. There was no in-between. There were a lot of better singers and better musicians around these places but there wasn't anybody close in nature to what I was doing. Folk songs were the way I explored the universe, they were pictures and the pictures were worth more than anything I could say. . . . Most of the other performers tried to put themselves across, rather than the song, but I didn't care about doing that. With me, it was about putting the song across. (p. 26–27)

The madly complicated modern world was something I took little interest in. It had no relevancy, no weight. I wasn't seduced by it. What was swinging, topical and up to date for me was stuff like the Titanic sinking, the Galveston flood, John Henry driving steel, John Hardy shooting a man on the West Virginia line. All this was current, played out and in the open. This was the news that I considered, followed and kept tabs on. (p. 28)

Songs about debauched bootleggers, mothers that drowned their own children, Cadillacs that only got five miles to the gallon, floods, union hall fires, darkness and cadavers at the bottom of rivers weren't for radiophiles. There was nothing easygoing about the folk songs I sang. They weren't friendly or ripe with mellowness. They didn't come gently

---

[37]   BOB DYLAN *Chronicles*, Volume One, Simon & Schuster, 2004.

to the shore. I guess you could say they weren't commercial. (p. 42–43)

The folksingers could sing songs like an entire book, but only in a few verses. It's hard to describe what makes a character or an event folk song worthy. It probably has something to do with a character being fair and honest and open. Bravery in an abstract way. (p. 47–48)

I needed to learn how to telescope things, ideas. Things were too big to see all at once, like all the books in the library—everything laying around on all the tables. You might be able to put it all into one paragraph or into one verse of a song if you could get it right. (p. 70)

Latin artists were breaking rules, too. Artists like João Gilberto, Roberto Menescal and Carlos Lyra were breaking away from the drum infested samba stuff and creating a new form of Brazilian music with melodic changes. They were calling it bossa nova. As for me, what I did to break away was to take simple folk changes and put new imagery and attitude to them, use catchphrases and metaphor combined with a new set of ordinances that evolved into something different that had not been heard before. (p. 75–76)

What I was going to do as soon as I left home was just call myself Robert Allen. As far as I was concerned, that was who I was—that's what my parents named me. It sounded like the name of a Scottish king and I liked it. There was little of my identity that wasn't in it. What kind of confused me later was seeing an article in a Downbeat magazine with a story about a West Coast saxophone player named David Allyn. I had suspected that the musician had changed the spelling of Allen to Allyn. I could see why. It looked more exotic, more inscrutable. I was going to do this, too. Instead of Robert Allen it would be Robert Allyn. Then sometime later, unexpectedly, I'd seen some poems by Dylan Thomas. Dylan and Allyn sounded similar. Robert Dylan. Robert Allyn. I couldn't decide—the letter D came on stronger. But Robert Dylan didn't look or sound as good as Robert Allyn. People had always called me either Robert or Bobby, but Bobby Dylan sounded too skittish to me. . . . Bob Dylan looked and sounded better than Bob Allyn. The first time I was asked my name in the Twin Cities, I instinctively and automatically without thinking simply said, "Bob Dylan." (p. 86–87)

I did everything fast. Thought fast, ate fast, talked fast and walked fast. I even sang my songs fast. I needed to slow my mind down if I was going to be a composer with anything to say. (p. 92–93)

Newspapers like the Chicago Tribune, the Brooklyn Daily Times and the Pennsylvania Freeman. Others, too, like the Memphis Daily Eagle, the Savannah Daily Herald and Cincinnati Enquirer. . . . There were news items about reform movements, antigambling leagues, rising crime, child labor, temperance, slave-wage factories, loyalty oaths and religious revivals. You get the feeling that the newspapers themselves could explode and lightning will burn and everybody will perish. (p. 93)

The big bugs in the press kept promoting me as the mouthpiece, spokesman, or even conscience of a generation. That was funny. All I'd ever done was sing songs that were dead straight and expressed powerful new realities. (p. 123)

Joan Baez recorded a protest song about me that was getting big play, challenging me to get with it—come out and take charge, lead the masses—be an advocate, lead the crusade. The song called out to me from the radio like a public service announcement. (p. 127)

I was sick of the way my lyrics had been extrapolated, their meanings subverted into polemics and that I had been anointed as the Big Bubba of Rebellion, High Priest of Protest, the Czar of Dissent, the Duke of Disobedience, Leader of the Freeloaders, Kaiser of Apostasy, Archbishop of Anarchy, the Big Cheese. What the hell are we talking about? Horrible titles any way you want to look at it. (p. 128)

In the studio the songs had only been sketched out but never brought from the shadows. There'd always been too many problems—wrestling with lyric phrasing, changing lyrics, switching melody lines, keys, tempos, any number of things all the while searching for a song's stylistic identity. (p. 168–169)

A song is like a dream, and you try to make it come true. They're like strange countries that you have to enter. You can write a song anywhere, in a railroad compartment, on a boat, on horseback—it helps to be moving. (p. 174)

I laid down, listened to the crickets and wildlife out the window in the eerie blackness. I liked the night. Things grow at night. My imagination is available to me at night. All my preconceptions of things go away. Sometimes you could be looking for heaven in the wrong places. Sometimes it could be under your feet. Or in your bed. (p. 210–211)

Woody's got a fierce poetic soul—the poet of hard crust sod and gumbo mud. Guthrie divides the world between those who work and those who don't and is interested in the liberation of the human race and wants to create a world worth living in. (p. 253–254)

I began singing them all, felt connected to these songs on every level. They were cosmic. One thing for sure, Woody Guthrie had never seen nor heard of me, but it felt like he was saying, "I'll be going away, but I'm leaving this job in your hands. I know I can count on you." (p. 254–255)

A lot of folks might have thought of Woody's songs as backdated, but not me. I felt they were totally in the moment, current and even forecasted things to come. I felt anything but like the young punk folksinger who had just begun out of nowhere six months previously. It felt more like I had instantly risen up from a noncommissioned volunteer to an honorable knight—stripes and gold stars. (p. 256)

The folk and blues tunes had already given me my proper concept of culture, and now with Guthrie's songs my heart and mind had been sent into another cosmological place of that culture entirely. (p. 256)

4

I Is Another:
Bob Dylan's Quotes[38]

1. Take care of all your memories. For you cannot relive them.
2. All the truth in the world adds up to one big lie.
3. To live outside the law, you must be honest.
4. You're going to die. You're going to be dead. It could be twenty years, it could be tomorrow, anytime. So am I. I mean, we're just going to be gone. The world's going to go on without us. All right now. You do your job in the face of that, and how seriously you take yourself you decide for yourself.
5. Chaos is a friend of mine.
6. Well, the future for me is already a thing of the past.
7. I paint mostly from real life. It has to start with that. Real people, real street scenes, behind-the-curtain scenes, live models, paintings, photographs, staged setups, architecture, grids, and graphic design. Whatever it takes to make it work.
8. A hero is someone who understands the responsibility that comes with his freedom.
9. Democracy don't rule the world, You'd better get that in your head; This world is ruled by violence, But I guess that's better left unsaid.
10. Being noticed can be a burden. Jesus got himself crucified because he got himself noticed. So, I disappear a lot.

---

38 https://www.brainyquote.com/search_results?q=bob+dylan

11. I like America, just as everybody else does. I love America, I gotta say that. But America will be judged.
12. I say there're no depressed words just depressed minds.
13. I can be jubilant one moment and pensive the next, and a cloud could go by and make that happen.
14. No one is free, even the birds are chained to the sky.
15. All I can do is be me, whoever that is.
16. Money doesn't talk, it swears.
17. People seldom do what they believe in. They do what is convenient, then repent.
18. At times in my life the only place I have been happy is when I am on stage.
19. Basically, you have to suppress your own ambitions in order to be who you need to be.
20. I don't think the human mind can comprehend the past and the future. They are both just illusions that can manipulate you into thinking there's some kind of change.
21. I don't think I've ever been an agnostic. I've always thought there's a superior power, that this is not the real world, and that there's a world to come.
22. I'm mortified to be on the stage, but then again, it's the only place where I'm happy.
23. It's not easy to define poetry.
24. Being on tour is like being in limbo. It's like going from nowhere to nowhere.
25. A lot of people don't like the road, but it's as natural to me as breathing.
26. The people in my songs are all me.

27. Death to me means nothing as long as I can die fast.

28. Nothing can affect my voice, it's so bad.

29. My songs always sound a lot better in person than they do on the record.

30. I can't act!

5

The Sun Continues to Shine

HAVING STUDIED BOB DYLAN'S great body of work, I decided to divide it into three key periods: dawn, sunset, and new morning.

In my opinion, the dawn of the songwriter began in 1962 with the release of his first album and stretched all the way to when he embraced Christianity in the late seventies. His sunset ended when he met Pope John Paul II in 1997, while the new morning ended with his involvement in the intoxicating Heaven's Door whiskey.

As I initially said, Dylan stood out for his dynamic and subversive protest songs. But in the 1980s, with the appearance of MTV—a music channel that emphasized music videos rather than the songs themselves—Dylan's star began to sink on the horizon.

Giant advertising companies entered a nonstop competition over who would promote their products, seeking artists with mass appeal and influence, such as Madonna and Michael Jackson. With viewers' eyes fixed on television sets, unfortunately or fortunately, entertainment took on a much fancier form. What role could a forty-five-year-old man, with his tobacco-rough voice and songs about social justice and political changes, play in the era of pop and disco music? After a long period of introspection trying to find his footing again, Dylan performed on *MTV Unplugged* in 1994. His star began to shine again.

The period of his new morning soon followed, taking him all the way to the celebrated Stockholm awards and emphasizing his role as prophet in his seeming prediction of September 11 ("Mississippi"), Hurricane Katrina ("High Water"), and the global financial crisis of

2008 ("Workingman's Blues #2"). But let us not forget that we live in a postmodern era. Thus, Dylan's third period, although without a doubt of great musical and poetic interest, was also characterized by a mood of commercial lightness.

For example, in the last, iconic scene of the movie *Wonder Boys*, Dylan munches on a hamburger from a fast-food joint, then gives a sly wink at the camera before singing "Things Have Changed." It's as if he is telling us that once upon a time, he cared, but now things have changed. While he began his career with hopes, ambitions, goals, and objectives, things are not as he once imagined they would be. Despite his best efforts and his countless struggles for a better and fairer world, he is deeply disappointed with what has emerged.

Much to my surprise, in 2004 he came out with "Lovesick" for Victoria's Secret's TV spot, alongside Brazilian beauty Adriana Lima, advertising sexy women's underwear. Five years later, he released an album of Christmas songs and gave the profits to the homeless and people in need. In the music video of "Must Be Santa," we see him dressed as Santa Claus, having great fun.

In 2014 he surprised me again, appearing in an advertising campaign for Chrysler cars that was loaded with American pride. In the commercial, he enters a billiard room and, holding the cue as an experienced player, he tells us in his hoarse voice: "We will build your car!"[39]

Finally, the following year, he arranged songs by his favorite singer, Frank Sinatra, who liked to hang out at bars and disappear into the blue shadows of the night. Frank once said, "Alcohol can be man's worst enemy, but the Bible says to love your enemy."[40]

---

39 https://www.hollywoodreporter.com/news/general-news/bob-dylan-super-bowl-chrysler-676570/
40 https://www.goodreads.com/quotes/7670-alcohol-may-be-man-s-worst-enemy-but-the-bible-says

PART TWO

"The Bible is very resonant. It has everything: creation, betrayal, lust, poetry, prophecy, sacrifice. All great things are in the Bible, and all great writers have drawn from it and more than people realise, whether Shakespeare, Herman Melville or Bob Dylan."[41]

PATTI SMITH

---
41 https://www.brainyquote.com/quotes/patti_smith_733356?src=t_bob_dylan

6

Are My Songs Literature?

EVEN THOUGH BOB DYLAN became the first songwriter in the history of the Swedish Academy to be awarded the Nobel Prize in Literature in 2016, he did not go to the award ceremony in early December, causing not only surprise but also irritation. Many did not hesitate to characterize his behavior as indecent and arrogant.

However, Dylan did send a humble thank-you letter, which the United States ambassador in Stockholm, Azita Raji, read on his behalf. The letter reads:[42]

> Good evening, everyone. I extend my warmest greetings to the members of the Swedish Academy and to all of the other distinguished guests in attendance tonight.
>
> I'm sorry I can't be with you in person, but please know that I am most definitely with you in spirit and honored to be receiving such a prestigious prize. Being awarded the Nobel Prize in Literature is something I never could have imagined or seen coming. From an early age, I've been familiar with and reading and absorbing the works of those who were deemed worthy of such a distinction: Kipling, Shaw, Thomas Mann, Pearl Buck, Albert Camus, and Hemingway. These giants of literature whose works are taught in the schoolroom, housed in libraries around the world, and spoken of in reverent tones have always made a deep impression. That I now join the names on such a list is truly beyond words.

---

[42] https://www.nobelprize.org/prizes/literature/2016/dylan/speech/

I don't know if these men and women ever thought of the Nobel honor for themselves, but I suppose that anyone writing a book, a poem, or a play anywhere in the world might harbor that secret dream deep down inside. It's probably buried so deep that they don't even know it's there.

If someone had ever told me that I had the slightest chance of winning the Nobel Prize, I would have to think that I'd have about the same odds as standing on the moon. In fact, during the year I was born and for a few years after, there wasn't anyone in the world who was considered good enough to win this Nobel Prize. So, I recognize that I am in very rare company, to say the least.

I was out on the road when I received this surprising news, and it took me more than a few minutes to properly process it. I began to think about William Shakespeare, the great literary figure. I would reckon he thought of himself as a dramatist. The thought that he was writing literature couldn't have entered his head. His words were written for the stage. Meant to be spoken, not read. When he was writing Hamlet, I'm sure he was thinking about a lot of different things: "Who are the right actors for these roles?" "How should this be staged?" "Do I really want to set this in Denmark?" His creative vision and ambitions were no doubt at the forefront of his mind, but there were also more mundane matters to consider and deal with. "Is the financing in place?" "Are there enough good seats for my patrons?" "Where am I going to get a human skull?" I would bet that the farthest thing from Shakespeare's mind was the question "Is this literature?"

When I started writing songs as a teenager, and even as I started to achieve some renown for my abilities, my aspirations for these songs only went so far. I thought they could be heard in coffee houses or bars, maybe later in places like Carnegie Hall and the London Palladium. If I was really dreaming big, maybe I could imagine getting to make a record and then hearing my songs on the radio. That was really the big prize in my mind. Making records and hearing your songs on the radio meant that you were reaching a big audience and that you might get to keep doing what you had set out to do.

Well, I've been doing what I set out to do for a long time, now. I've made dozens of records and played in thousands of concerts all around the world. But it's my songs that are at the vital center of almost everything I do. They seemed to have found a place in the lives of many people throughout many different cultures and I'm grateful for that.

But there's one thing I must say. As a performer, I've played for 50,000 people and I've played for 50 people, and I can tell you that it is harder to play for 50 people. 50,000 people have a singular persona—not so with 50. Each person has an individual, separate identity, a world unto themselves. They can perceive things more clearly. Your honesty and how it relates to the depth of your talent is tried. The fact that the Nobel committee is so small is not lost on me.

But, like Shakespeare, I too am often occupied with the pursuit of my creative endeavors and dealing with all aspects of life's mundane matters. "Who are the best musicians for these songs?" "Am I recording in the right studio?" "Is this song in the right key?" Some things never change, even in 400 years.

Not once have I ever had the time to ask myself, "Are my songs literature?"

So, I do thank the Swedish Academy, both for taking the time to consider that very question, and, ultimately, for providing such a wonderful answer.

My best wishes to you all.

In the place of the troubadour, Patti Smith sang "A Hard Rain's A-Gonna Fall," accompanied by an orchestra. It is worth noting that Patti, because of her nerves, sang the wrong words at one point, but she picked the song up again and completed it, winning warm applause from the audience.

An award winner's inability to attend the ceremony is unusual but not unheard of. This happened with the writer Harold Pinder, who did not show up because of health reasons, while the Austrian Elfriede Jelinek refused to travel to Scandinavia because he suffered from agoraphobia. The British Doris Lessing, who won the Nobel in 2007, wrote a speech and sent it to her Swedish editor.

However, the following spring, in a hoodie and black leather jacket, Bob Dylan crossed the Atlantic for a concert in Stockholm and went to collect his award behind closed doors, with the media nowhere in sight. According to Dylan's wishes, in the room were only a few committee members and academics. Dylan hadn't given a lecture, raising questions about whether he would exhaust the deadline for receiving the prize money, which was supposed to be given to him in early June.

When a journalist asked if the borders in the world of literature were being expanded, the then secretary of the Swedish Academy, Sarah Danius (1962–2019), answered, "If you think back to Homer and Sappho, you realise that was also aural poetry. It was meant to be performed, together with instruments. But we still read them, 2,500-some years later. . . . And in much the same way you can read Bob Dylan too. And you realise that he is great at rhyming, great at putting together refrains and great at poetic images."[43]

---

43   https://newcriterion.com/issues/2016/11/homer-sappho-dylan

7

The Dylan Adventure Is Coming to an End

I'M SURE WE can all picture Dylan entering a recording studio in the City of Angels, sitting in front of a microphone, putting on his headphones, taking a sip of whiskey, and then beginning to read what he wants to say about the award.

The Nobel situation was not the first time Dylan was invited to accept an award from a prestigious institution. Near the dawn of the 1970s, he accepted an honorary doctorate in music from Princeton University. The event was organized exclusively for him, and afterward he wrote the song "Day of the Locusts," which tells us that after all the embarrassment, the normally private musician finally managed to get out of the event in one piece.

Sarah Danius said of the lecture Dylan had been required to give within six months of receiving the prize in order to receive the money: "The speech is excellent and, as one might expect, elegant. Now that the lecture has been delivered, the Dylan adventure is coming to a close."[44]

∽

Nobel Lecture Speech[45]
June 5, 2017

When I first received this Nobel Prize for Literature, I got to wondering exactly how my songs related to literature. I

---

[44] https://www.timesofisrael.com/bob-dylan-ponders-literary-links-in-extraordinary-nobel-speech/
[45] https://www.youtube.com/watch?v=6TlcPRlau2Q&t=6s

wanted to reflect on it and see where the connection was. I'm going to try to articulate that to you. And most likely it will go in a roundabout way, but I hope what I say will be worthwhile and purposeful.

If I was to go back to the dawning of it all, I guess I'd have to start with Buddy Holly. Buddy died when I was about eighteen and he was twenty-two. From the moment I first heard him, I felt akin. I felt related like he was an older brother. I even thought I resembled him. Buddy played the music that I loved—the music I grew up on, country western, rock 'n' roll, and rhythm and blues. Three separate strands of music that he intertwined and infused into one genre. One brand. And Buddy wrote songs—songs that had beautiful melodies and imaginative verses. And he sang great—sang in more than a few voices. He was the archetype. Everything I wasn't and wanted to be. I saw him only once, and that was a few days before he was gone. I had to travel a hundred miles to get to see him play, and I wasn't disappointed.

He was powerful and electrifying and had a commanding presence. I was only six feet away. He was mesmerizing. I watched his face, his hands, the way he tapped his foot, his big black glasses, the eyes behind the glasses, the way he held his guitar, the way he stood, and his neat suit. Everything about him. He looked older than twenty-two. Something about him seemed permanent, and he filled me with conviction. Then, out of the blue, the most uncanny thing happened. He looked me right straight dead in the eye, and he transmitted something. Something I didn't know what. And it gave me the chills.

I think it was a day or two after that that his plane went down. And somebody—somebody I'd never seen before—handed me a Lead Belly record with the song "Cottonfields" on it. And that record changed my life right then and there. Transported me into a world I'd never known. It was like an explosion went off. Like I'd been walking in darkness and all of a sudden the darkness was illuminated. It was like somebody laid hands on me. I must have played that record a hundred times.

It was on a label I'd never heard of with a booklet inside with advertisements for other artists on the label: Sonny Terry and Brownie McGhee, the New Lost City Ramblers, Jean Ritchie, and string bands. I'd never heard of any of them. But I reckoned if they were on this label with Lead Belly, they had to be good, so I needed to hear them. I wanted to know all about it and play that kind of music. I still had a feeling for the music I'd grown up with, but for right now, I forgot about it. Didn't even think about it. For the time being, it was long gone.

I hadn't left home yet, but I couldn't wait to. I wanted to learn this music and meet the people who played it. Eventually, I did leave, and I did learn to play those songs. They were different from the radio songs that I'd been listening to all along. They were more vibrant and truthful to life. With radio songs, a performer might get a hit with a roll of the dice or a fall of the cards, but that didn't matter in the folk world. Everything was a hit. All you had to do was be well-versed and be able to play the melody. Some of these songs were easy, some not. I had a natural feeling for the ancient ballads and country blues, but everything else I had to learn from scratch. I was playing for small crowds, sometimes no more than four or five people in a room or on a street corner. You had to have a wide repertoire, and you had to know what to play and when. Some songs were intimate, some you had to shout to be heard.

By listening to all the early folk artists and singing the songs yourself, you pick up the vernacular. You internalize it. You sing it in the ragtime blues, work songs, Georgia sea shanties, the Appalachian ballads and cowboy songs. You hear all the finer points, and you learn the details.

You know what it's all about. Takin' the pistol out and puttin' it back in your pocket. Whippin' your way through traffic, talkin' in the dark. You know that Stagger Lee was a bad man and that Frankie was a good girl. You know that Washington is a bourgeois town and you've heard the deep-pitched voice of John the Revelator and you saw the *Titanic* sink in a boggy creek. And you're pals with the wild Irish rover and the wild colonial boy. You heard the muffled drums and the fifes that played lowly. You've seen the lusty Lord Donald stick a knife in his wife, and a lot of your comrades have been wrapped in white linen.

I had all the vernacular down. I knew the rhetoric. None of it went over my head—the devices, the techniques, the secrets, the mysteries—and I knew all the deserted roads that it traveled on, too. I could make it all connect and move with the current of the day. When I started writing my own songs, the folk lingo was the only vocabulary that I knew, and I used it.

But I had something else as well. I had principles and sensibilities and an informed view of the world. And I had had that for a while. Learned it all in grammar school. *Don Quixote, Ivanhoe, Robinson Crusoe, Gulliver's Travels, Tale of Two Cities,* all the rest—typical grammar school reading that gave you a way of looking at life, an understanding of human nature, and a standard to measure things by. I took all that with me when I started composing lyrics. And the themes from those books worked their way into many of my songs, either knowingly or unintentionally. I wanted to write songs unlike anything anybody ever heard, and these themes were fundamental.

Specific books that have stuck with me ever since I read them way back in grammar school—I want to tell you about three of them: *Moby Dick, All Quiet on the Western Front* and *The Odyssey.*

Moby Dick is a fascinating book, a book that's filled with scenes of high drama and dramatic dialogue. The book makes demands on you. The plot is straightforward. The mysterious Captain Ahab—captain of a ship called the *Pequod*—an egomaniac with a peg leg pursuing his nemesis, the great white whale Moby Dick who took his leg. And he pursues him all the way from the Atlantic around the tip of Africa and into the Indian Ocean. He pursues the whale around both sides of the earth. It's an abstract goal, nothing concrete or definite. He calls Moby the emperor, sees him as the embodiment of evil. Ahab's got a wife and child back in Nantucket that he reminisces about now and again. You can anticipate what will happen.

The ship's crew is made up of men of different races, and any one of them who sights the whale will be given the reward of a gold coin. A lot of Zodiac symbols, religious allegory, stereotypes. Ahab encounters other whaling vessels, presses the captains for details about Moby. Have they seen him? There's a crazy prophet, Gabriel, on one of the vessels, and he predicts Ahab's doom. Says Moby is the incarnate of a Shaker god, and that any dealings with him will lead to disaster. He says that to Captain Ahab. Another ship's captain—Captain Boomer—he lost an arm to Moby. But he tolerates that, and he's happy to have survived. He can't accept Ahab's lust for vengeance.

This book tells how different men react in different ways to the same experience. A lot of Old Testament, biblical allegory: Gabriel, Rachel, Jeroboam, Bildah, Elijah. Pagan names as well: Tashtego, Flask, Daggoo, Fleece, Starbuck, Stubb, Martha's Vineyard. The Pagans are idol worshippers. Some worship little wax figures, some wooden figures. Some worship fire. The Pequod is the name of an Indian tribe.

Moby Dick is a seafaring tale. One of the men, the narrator, says, "Call me Ishmael." Somebody asks him where he's from, and he says, "It's not down on any map. True places never are." Stubb gives no significance to anything, says everything is predestined. Ishmael's been on a sailing ship his entire life. Calls the sailing ships his Harvard and Yale. He keeps his distance from people.

A typhoon hits the *Pequod*. Captain Ahab thinks it's a good omen. Starbuck thinks it's a bad omen, considers killing Ahab. As soon as the storm ends, a crewmember falls from the ship's mast and drowns, foreshadowing what's to come. A Quaker pacifist priest, who is actually a bloodthirsty businessman, tells Flask, "Some men who receive injuries are led to God, others are led to bitterness."

Everything is mixed in. All the myths: the Judeo-Christian bible, Hindu myths, British legends, Saint George, Perseus, Hercules—they're all whalers. Greek mythology, the gory business of cutting up a whale. Lots of facts in this book, geographical knowledge, whale oil—good for coronation of royalty—noble families in the whaling industry. Whale oil is used to anoint the kings. History of the whale, phrenology, classical philosophy, pseudo-scientific theories, justification for discrimination—everything thrown in and none of it hardly rational. Highbrow, lowbrow, chasing illusion, chasing death, the great white whale, white as polar bear, white as a white man, the emperor, the nemesis, the embodiment of evil. The demented captain who actually lost his leg years ago trying to attack Moby with a knife.

We see only the surface of things. We can interpret what lies below any way we see fit. Crewmen walk around on deck listening for mermaids, and sharks and vultures follow the ship. Reading skulls and faces like you read a book. Here's a face. I'll put it in front of you. Read it if you can.

Tashtego says that he died and was reborn. His extra days

are a gift. He wasn't saved by Christ, though, he says he was saved by a fellow man and a non-Christian at that. He parodies the resurrection.

When Starbuck tells Ahab that he should let bygones be bygones, the angry captain snaps back, "Speak not to me of blasphemy, man, I'd strike the sun if it insulted me." Ahab, too, is a poet of eloquence. He says, "The path to my fixed purpose is laid with iron rails whereon my soul is grooved to run." Or these lines, "All visible objects are but pasteboard masks." Quotable poetic phrases that can't be beat.

Finally, Ahab spots Moby, and the harpoons come out. Boats are lowered. Ahab's harpoon has been baptized in blood. Moby attacks Ahab's boat and destroys it. Next day, he cites Moby again. Boats are lowered again. Moby attacks Ahab's boat again. On the third day, another boat goes in. More religious allegory. He has risen. Moby attacks one more time, ramming the Pequod and sinking it. Ahab gets tangled up in the harpoon lines and is thrown out of his boat into a watery grave.

Ishmael survives. He's in the sea floating on a coffin. And that's about it. That's the whole story. That theme and all that it implies would work its way into more than a few of my songs.

All Quiet on the Western Front was another book that did. *All Quiet on the Western Front* is a horror story. This is a book where you lose your childhood, your faith in a meaningful world, and your concern for individuals. You're stuck in a nightmare. Sucked up into a mysterious whirlpool of death and pain. You're defending yourself from elimination. You're being wiped off the face of the map. Once upon a time, you were an innocent youth with big dreams about being a concert pianist. Once you loved life and the world, and now you're shooting it to pieces.

Day after day, the hornets bite you and worms lap your

blood. You're a cornered animal. You don't fit anywhere. The falling rain is monotonous. There's endless assaults, poison gas, nerve gas, morphine, burning streams of gasoline, scavenging and scabbing for food, influenza, typhus, dysentery. Life is breaking down all around you, and the shells are whistling. This is the lower region of hell. Mud, barbed wire, rat-filled trenches, rats eating the intestines of dead men, trenches filled with filth and excrement. Someone shouts, "Hey, you there. Stand and fight."

Who knows how long this mess will go on? Warfare has no limits. You're being annihilated, and that leg of yours is bleeding too much. You killed a man yesterday, and you spoke to his corpse. You told him after this is over, you'll spend the rest of your life looking after his family. Who's profiting here? The leaders and the generals gain fame, and many others profit financially. But you're doing the dirty work. One of your comrades says, "Wait a minute, where are you going?" And you say, "Leave me alone. I'll be back in a minute." Then you walk out into the woods of death hunting for a piece of sausage. You can't see how anybody in civilian life has any kind of purpose at all. All their worries, all their desires, you can't comprehend it.

More machine guns rattle, more parts of bodies hanging from wires, more pieces of arms and legs and skulls where butterflies perch on teeth, more hideous wounds, pus coming out of every pore, lung wounds, wounds too big for the body, gas-blowing cadavers, and dead bodies making retching noises. Death is everywhere. Nothing else is possible. Someone will kill you and use your dead body for target practice. Boots, too. They're your prized possession. But soon they'll be on somebody else's feet.

There's Froggies coming through the trees. Merciless bastards. Your shells are running out. "It's not fair to come at us again so soon," you say. One of your companions is laying in the dirt, and you want to take him to the field hospital. Someone else says, "You might save yourself a trip." "What do you mean?" "Turn him over, you'll see what I mean."

You wait to hear the news. You don't understand why the war isn't over. The army is so strapped for replacement troops that they're drafting young boys who are of little military use, but they're draftin' 'em anyway because they're running out of men. Sickness and humiliation have broken your heart. You were betrayed by your parents, your schoolmasters, your ministers, and even your own government.

The general with the slowly smoked cigar betrayed you too—turned you into a thug and a murderer. If you could, you'd put a bullet in his face. The commander as well. You fantasize that if you had the money, you'd put up a reward for any man who would take his life by any means necessary. And if he should lose his life by doing that, then let the money go to his heirs. The colonel, too, with his caviar and his coffee—he's another one. Spends all his time in the officers' brothel. You'd like to see him stoned dead too. More Tommies and Johnnies with their whack fo' me daddy-o and their whiskey in the jars. You kill twenty of 'em and twenty more will spring up in their place. It just stinks in your nostrils.

You've come to despise that older generation that sent you out into this madness, into this torture chamber. All around you, your comrades are dying. Dying from abdominal wounds, double amputations, shattered hipbones, and you think, *I'm only twenty years old, but I'm capable of killing anybody. Even my father if he came at me.*

Yesterday, you tried to save a wounded messenger dog, and somebody shouted, "Don't be a fool." One Froggy is laying gurgling at your feet. You stuck him with a dagger in his stomach, but the man still lives. You know you should finish the job, but you can't. You're on the real iron cross, and a Roman soldier's putting a sponge of vinegar to your lips.

Months pass by. You go home on leave. You can't communicate with your father. He said, "You'd be a coward if you don't enlist." Your mother, too, on your way back out the door, she says, "You be careful of those French girls now." More madness. You fight for a week or a month, and you gain ten yards. And then the next month it gets taken back.

All that culture from a thousand years ago, that philosophy, that wisdom—Plato, Aristotle, Socrates—what happened to it? It should have prevented this. Your thoughts turn homeward. And once again you're a schoolboy walking through the tall poplar trees. It's a pleasant memory. More bombs dropping on you from blimps. You got to get it together now. You can't even look at anybody for fear of some miscalculating thing that might happen. The common grave. There are no other possibilities.

Then you notice the cherry blossoms, and you see that nature is unaffected by all this. Poplar trees, the red butterflies, the fragile beauty of flowers, the sun—you see how nature is indifferent to it all. All the violence and suffering of all mankind. Nature doesn't even notice it.

You're so alone. Then a piece of shrapnel hits the side of your head and you're dead. You've been ruled out, crossed out. You've been exterminated. I put this book down and closed it up. I never wanted to read another war novel again, and I never did.

Charlie Poole from North Carolina had a song that connected to all this. It's called "You Ain't Talkin' to Me," and the lyrics go like this:

I saw a sign in a window walking uptown one day.
Join the army, see the world is what it had to say.
You'll see exciting places with a jolly crew,

You'll meet interesting people, and learn to kill them too.
Oh you ain't talkin' to me, you ain't talking to me.
I may be crazy and all that, but I got good sense you see.
You ain't talkin' to me, you ain't talkin' to me.
Killin' with a gun don't sound like fun.
You ain't talkin' to me.

The Odyssey is a great book whose themes have worked its way into the ballads of a lot of songwriters: "Homeward Bound, "Green, Green Grass of Home," "Home on the Range," and my songs as well.

The Odyssey is a strange, adventurous tale of a grown man trying to get home after fighting in a war. He's on that long journey home, and it's filled with traps and pitfalls. He's cursed to wander. He's always getting carried out to sea, always having close calls. Huge chunks of boulders rock his boat. He angers people he shouldn't. There are troublemakers in his crew. Treachery. His men are turned into pigs and then are turned back into younger, more handsome men. He's always trying to rescue somebody. He's a travelin' man, but he's making a lot of stops.

He's stranded on a desert island. He finds deserted caves, and he hides in them. He meets giants that say, "I'll eat you last." And he escapes from the giants. He's trying to get back home, but he's tossed and turned by the winds. Restless winds, chilly winds, unfriendly winds. He travels far, and then he gets blown back.

He's always being warned of things to come. Touching things, he's told not to. There're two roads to take, and they're both bad. Both hazardous. On one you could drown and on the other, you could starve. He goes into the narrow straits with foaming whirlpools that swallow him. Meets six-headed monsters with sharp fangs. Thunderbolts strike at him. Overhanging branches that he makes a leap to reach for to save himself from a raging river. Goddesses and gods protect him, but some others wanna kill him. He changes identities. He's exhausted. He falls asleep, and he's woken up by the sound of laughter. He tells his story to strangers. He's been gone twenty years. He was carried off somewhere and left there. Drugs have been dropped into his wine. It's been a hard road to travel.

In a lot of ways, some of these same things have happened to you. You too have had drugs dropped into your wine. You too have shared a bed with the wrong woman. You too have been spellbound by magical voices, sweet voices with strange melodies. You too have come so far and have been so far blown back. And you've had close calls as well. You have angered people you should not have. And you too have rambled this country all around. And you've also felt that ill wind, the one that blows you no good. And that's still not all of it.

When he gets back home, things aren't any better. Scoundrels have moved in and are taking advantage of his wife's hospitality. And there's too many of 'em. And though he's greater than them all and the best at everything—best carpenter, best hunter, best expert on animals, best seaman—his courage won't save him, his trickery will.

All these stragglers will have to pay for desecrating his palace. He'll disguise himself as a filthy beggar, and a lowly servant kicks him down the steps with arrogance and stupidity. The servant's arrogance revolts him, but he controls his anger. He's one against a hundred, but they'll all fall, even the strongest. He was nobody. And when it's all said and done when he's home, at last, he sits with his wife, and he tells her the stories.

So, what does it all mean? A lot of other songwriters and I, we have been influenced by these very same themes. And they can mean a lot of different things. If a song moves you, that's all that's important. I don't have to know what a song means.

I've written all kinds of things into my songs. And I'm not going to worry about it—what it all means. When Melville put all his Old Testament, biblical references, scientific theories, Protestant doctrines, and all that knowledge of the sea and sailing ships and whales into one story, I don't think he would have worried about it either—what it all means.

John Donne as well, the poet-priest who lived in the time of Shakespeare, wrote these words, "The Sestos and Abydos of her breasts. Not of two lovers, but two loves, the nests." I don't know what it means, either. But it sounds good. And you want your songs to sound good.

When Odysseus in *The Odyssey* visits the famed warrior Achilles in the underworld—Achilles, who traded a long life full of peace and contentment for a short one full of honor and glory—tells Odysseus it was all a mistake. "I just died, that's all." There was no honor. No immortality. And that if he could, he would choose to go back and be a lowly slave to a tenant farmer on Earth rather than be what he is—a king in the land of the dead—that whatever his struggles of life were, they were preferable to being here in this dead place.

That's what songs are too. Our songs are alive in the land of the living. But songs are unlike literature. They're meant to be sung, not read. The words in Shakespeare's plays were meant to be acted on the stage. Just as lyrics in songs are meant to be sung, not read on a page. And I hope some of you get the chance to listen to these lyrics the way they were intended to be heard in concert or on record or however people are listening to songs these days. I return once again to Homer, who says, "Sing in me, oh Muse, and through me tell the story."

∼

Against the backdrop of a jazzy, cocktail-bar piano, Bob Dylan began by reflecting on how his songs relate to literature, and for those who were critical of Dylan's Nobel win, this cut to the chase. After a brief sketch of his musical influences, Dylan moved on to literature. Just as with his singing, there was something magnetic, hypnotic, and mystical about Dylan's Nobel speech delivery.

First, he talked about the novel *Moby Dick* by Herman Melville, published in 1851. The narrator of the book, Ishmael, eloquently describes the obsessive quest of Ahab, captain of the wailing ship *Pequod*. Ahab wants revenge against a giant sperm white whale that bit off his leg at the knee. Many scholars consider the novel to be a masterpiece of American literature, and they do not hesitate to compare it with the ancient Greek tragedies and the plays of Shakespeare.

Dylan then discussed *All Quiet on the West Front*, written by the German Erich Maria Remarque. The book, published in 1929, gained a reputation as an important antiwar story. Remarque describes his experiences during the First World War:[46] "We were eighteen and had begun to love life and the world; and we had to shoot it to pieces. The first bomb, the first explosion, burst in our hearts. We are cut off from activity, from striving, from progress. We believe in such things no longer, we believe in the war," he wrote. The main question he raises in the story is whether the enemy is in front of us or behind us.

Near the end of his speech, Dylan referred to the *Odyssey* and Homer and invoked the muse, which normally forms the introductory prologue of an epic, in place of an epilogue. Calliope is the patroness of poetry and the noblest of the nine muses. In the old days, the invocation to the goddess was a religious necessity and had a ritualistic character. This act was part of the tradition adopted by all the αηδούς during the ancient time. (The Greek word "*aoidos*" refers to a classical Greek singer.)

As expected, Dylan's lecture provoked many positive and negative reactions. Some did not hesitate to express their opinion that the troubadour used a study guide to compose and complete his speech. More

---

46 https://www.goodreads.com/quotes/136224-we-were-eighteen-and-had-begun-to-love-life-and

specifically, *Slate* magazine reported that excerpts from his lecture were pulled from SparkNotes (a website that offers analysis of literary works). This intrigue was probably initiated by a writer who accidentally discovered that some expressions from Dylan's speech related to *Moby Dick* were not in Melville's book but rather on the SparkNotes website.

Slate compared Dylan to a high school student who, after being taught classic literature in the classroom, must go home and study the material carefully and then complete his work by adding a few of his own thoughts to get a good grade. Surely this was not the first time something like this had happened. For decades, many suspected that Dylan incorporated texts by other authors into his lyrics, something which can be traced even in *Chronicles: Volume One*. In fact, many analysts do not know what to call him: a troubadour of adaptation or Arsène Lupin? Such accusations acquire a completely different meaning when someone has won the Nobel Prize in Literature.

Scott Warmuth, a writer and radio producer from New Mexico, noted in the *New York Times*[47] that many words and phrases in the album *"Love and Theft"* were lifted from *Confessions of a Yakuza* by Dr. Junichi Saga, which is about the life of a Japanese gangster. The same thing is noticeable with regard to the album *Modern Times*, with many songs including phrases from Henry Timrod, a nineteenth-century poet.

Author and researcher David Kinney, who deals with artistic similarities, in his book *The Dylanologists: Adventures in the Land of Bob* agrees[48] with Warmuth's opinion, while Joni Mitchell told the *Los Angeles Times* in 2014, "Bob is not authentic at all. He's a plagiarist, and his name and voice are fake."[49]

On the other hand, Jon Pareles, an American journalist and the

---

47 https://www.nytimes.com/2006/09/15/learning/featuredarticle/20060915friday.html
48 https://www.spin.com/2014/05/bob-dylan-da-vinci-code-chronicles-memoir-dylanologists-plagiarism/
49 https://www.theguardian.com/music/2010/apr/23/bob-dylan-joni-mitchell

chief popular music critic in the arts section of the *New York Times*, writes, "The hoopla over 'Love and Theft' and 'Confessions of a Yakuza' is a symptom of a growing misunderstanding about culture's ownership and evolution, a misunderstanding that has accelerated as humanity's oral tradition migrates to the Internet. Ideas aren't meant to be carved in stone and left inviolate; they're meant to stimulate the next idea and the next."[50]

In response to the accusations, Dylan told *Rolling Stone* magazine in 2012, "In folk and jazz, quotation is a rich and enriching tradition. That certainly is true. It's true for everybody but me. There are different rules for me. And as far as Henry Timrod is concerned, have you ever heard of him? Who's been reading him lately? And who's pushed him to the forefront? Who's been making you read him? And ask his descendants what they think of the hoopla. And if you think it's so easy to quote him and it can help your work, do it yourself and see how far you can get."[51]

"Wussies and pussies complain about that stuff," Dylan goes on. "It's an old thing—it's part of the tradition. It goes way back. These are the same people that tried to pin the name Judas on me. Judas is the most hated name in human history! If you think you've been called a bad name, try to work your way out from under that. Yeah, and for what? For playing an electric guitar? As if that is in some kind of way equitable to betraying our Lord and delivering him up to be crucified. All those evil motherfuckers can rot in hell."[52]

And he sums it all up by saying, "I'm working within my art form. It's that simple. I work within the rules and limitations of it. There are authoritarian figures that can explain that kind of art form better to you than I can. It's called songwriting. It has to do with melody and rhythm, and then after that, anything goes. You make everything yours. We all do it."

---

50   https://www.nytimes.com/2003/07/12/books/critic-s-notebook-plagiarism-in-dylan-or-a-cultural-collage.html

51   https://www.thewrap.com/wussies-and-pussies-complain-about-plagiarism-says-bob-dylan-new-interview-56181/

52   https://www.hollywoodreporter.com/news/music-news/bob-dylan-responds-plagiarism-accusation-369896/

8

Does a Writer of Lyrics Deserve Such a Distinction?

ON THE DAY the Swedish Academy announced it would honor the troubadour with the Nobel Prize in Literature, alert critics began to shoot arrows at him dipped in vitriolic ink: "So then, the Swedish Academy that never honored Leo Tolstoy, Henrik Ibsen, Mark Twain, Franz Kafka, Anton Chekhov, Vladimir Nabokov, and Jorge Luis Borges, chose to honor Dylan,"[53] stated one anonymous Twitter user. Also, novelist Jodi Picoult sarcastically tweeted, "I'm happy for Bob Dylan. But does this mean I can win a Grammy?"[54]

The Swedish Academy replied that Irish playwright, critic, polemist, and political activist George Bernard Shaw won the Nobel Prize in Literature for his work in 1925 and eight years later won an Oscar for his screenplay *Pygmalion*.

Alex Shephard, senior editor of the *New Republic*, wrote: "THE SWEDISH ACADEMY WILL NOT STOP TROLLING PHILIP ROTH," and the American author Jeff Vander Meer said: "Category Error! Category Error! Alert! Category Error! Alert! Category Error!"[55]

Journalists, critics, and artists around the world churned out spiteful comments. The French journalist, biographer, and historian Pierre Assouline stated, "The decision of the Swedish Academy is contemptuous to writers," while novelist Anne North says in a *New*

---

[53] https://www.financialexpress.com/lifestyle/does-bob-dylan-deserve-the-nobel-prize-for-literature/419097/

[54] https://teachrock.org/lesson/love-theft-debating-bob-dylans-nobel-prize/?fbclid=IwAR3_NsyCwpOXb8odF7zMfnbCl65Dr7k_JMsz6xyUJSb2MZbm1KxCnT-PRyuE

[55] https://www.huffpost.com/entry/reactions-to-bob-dylan-nobel-prize_n_57ff9013e-4b0162c043a36c1

York Times article, "As reading declines around the world, literary prizes are more important than ever. . . . Awarding the Nobel Prize to a novelist or poet is a way of affirming that fiction and poetry still matter." According to her, "Mr. Dylan is a brilliant lyricist. Yes, he has written a book of prose poetry and an autobiography. Yes, it is possible to analyze his lyrics as poetry. But Mr. Dylan's writing is inseparable from his music. He is great because he is a great musician, and when the Nobel committee gives the literature prize to a musician, it misses the opportunity to honor a writer."[56]

Music critic Everett True writes on his website, "Bob Dylan winning a Nobel Prize for Literature says everything about the establishment's understanding of the appeal of popular music—i.e. it has none. . . . Bob Dylan winning a Nobel Prize for Literature is not a reflection of 2016 and is rather shabby really. Might as well give Trump the Nobel Peace Prize for services to women. Why not Nina Simone? Why not Beyoncé? Why not FILL IN YOUR OWN FUCKING NAME? Pathetic. Dr. True, 2016 (my doctorate was earned, not conferred)."[57]

Trainspotting creator Irvine Wells dared to say, "I'm a Dylan fan, but this is an ill-conceived nostalgia award wrenched from the rancid prostates of senile, gibbering hippies. If you're a 'music' fan, look it up in the dictionary. Then 'literature.' Then compare and contrast."[58] Satirical writer Gary Shteyngart said, "I totally get the Nobel committee. Reading books is hard."[59]

The British *Telegraph* published a scathing article written by journalist and historian Tim Stanley. Here are a few excerpts.[60]

Bob Dylan has been awarded the Nobel Prize for Literature.

---

56 https://teachrock.org/wp-content/uploads/Document-Set-2.pdf
57 https://everetttrue.wordpress.com/2016/10/13/bob-dylan-wins-the-nobel-prize-for-literature-some-facts/
58 https://theconversation.com/explainer-are-bob-dylans-songs-literature-67061
59 https://twitter.com/Shteyngart/status/786539556594003972
60 https://www.iefimerida.gr/news/294648/telegraph-o-kosmos-opoy-kerdizei-nompel-logotehnias-o-mpomp-ntilan-einai-aytos-poy-kanei

> Why not? If the Nobel Committee can give a peace prize to Henry Kissinger, then it can give a literature prize to a man who hasn't written any literature. . . .
>
> This is not a question of taste. Bob Dylan is a great folk artist, maybe the greatest alive. But the Nobel is supposed to be awarded not on the basis of what the public likes (if it were, Doris Lessing wouldn't have won it) but on ability matched by idealism. Dylan has both, but his body of work falls far short of that produced by past winners: Yeats, Gide, O'Neill, Solzhenitsyn, etc.

And he ends his article with

> I will be called a fogey, a snob, an elitist, etc. On this point, I don't care! The culture is demonstrably poorer than it was a few decades ago and this has an impact on politics. With each year, standards seem to slip and what was once considered absurd seems quite normal. And what is excellent is sadly forgotten. Where that all ends, I don't know. Perhaps a Nobel Prize in 2025 was awarded to Donald Trump for lyrical tweeting.

Pilling up on negative remarks, jazz critic and poet Philip Larkin said:[61] "If we remove Dylan's verse from its melodic surroundings, then as poetry it looks half-baked, half-finished, incomplete and without the possibility of taking off," while critic Ian Hamilton asked, "Do his lyrics work only supported by his wire-braided nostrils or are they great on paper too?"[62] To Larkin I say that what really counts in art is the result and whether it provokes reflection and emotion. When one watches *Oedipus Tyrannus*, it would be foolish to suggest that the choral sections and the pantomimes of the actors should be separated so the spectator can judge whether the poetry of the play is half-baked.

---

61 https://booksjournal.gr/kritikes/poiisi/3278-einai-o-dylan-poiitis
62 https://booksjournal.gr/kritikes/poiisi/3278-einai-o-dylan-poiitis

In her book *Performed Literature*,⁶³ the medievalist Betsy Bowden states that Dylan's songs are intended for the stage; they concern live performance and representation. Bowden claims that what Dylan writes are not poems but rather lyrics addressed to the listening ear and not the eye that reads. If one draws the words from the melody and special interpretive ability of Dylan, they lose their power.

Karl Ove Knausgaard, the Norwegian author, told the *Guardian*: "I'm very divided. I love that the novel committee opens up for other kinds of literature—lyrics and so on. I think that's brilliant. But knowing that Dylan is the same generation as Pynchon, Philip Roth, Cormac McCarthy, makes it very difficult for me to accept it. I think one of those three should have had it, really. But if they get it next year, it will be fine."⁶⁴

Fortunately, there is always a flip side to any story. Positive remarks by distinguished individuals and world-famous artists emerged as well. Sarah Danius, former secretary of the Swedish Academy, announced: "For having created new poetic expressions within the great American song tradition."

She continued: "We're really giving it to Bob Dylan as a great poet—that's the reason we awarded him the prize. He's a great poet in the great English tradition, stretching from Milton and Blake onwards. And he's a very interesting traditionalist, in a highly original way. Not just the written tradition, but also the oral one; not just high literature, but also low literature."⁶⁵

The controversial Salman Rushdie tweeted, "From Orpheus to Faiz, song & poetry have been closely linked. Dylan is the brilliant inheritor of the bardic tradition. Great choice."⁶⁶

In *Rolling Stone* magazine, the inexhaustible American writer

---

63   https://booksjournal.gr/kritikes/poiisi/3278-einai-o-dylan-poiitis
64   https://www.theguardian.com/music/2016/oct/17/nobel-prize-bob-dylan-unable-to-reach?fbclid=IwAR0c3wFuvx8I4sJTfOVK1lXinToFkF4MXmU-HbBrInN-lcw-KNRocyHKANMY
65   https://www.theguardian.com/books/2016/oct/13/bob-dylan-wins-2016-nobel-prize-in-literature
66   https://learningenglish.voanews.com/a/bob-dylan-nobel-prize/3549715.html

and godfather of horror, supernatural, and science fiction, Stephen King, expresses, "People complaining about his Nobel either don't understand or it's just a plain old case of sour grapes. I've seen several literary writers who have turned their noses up at the Dylan thing, like Gary Shteyngart. Well, I've got news for you, Gary: There are a lot of deserving writers who have never gotten the Nobel Prize. And Gary Shteyngart will probably be one of them. That's no reflection on his work. You have to rise to the level of a Faulkner if you're an American."[67] He adds that his love of the singer has filtered down generations of the King family: "My kids listen to Dylan, and so do my grandkids. That's three generations. That's real longevity and quality. Most people in pop music are like moths around a bug light; they circle for a while and then there's a bright flash and they're gone. Not Dylan."

Leonard Cohen stated, "It's like pinning a medal on Mount Everest for being the highest mountain,"[68] while Tom Waits added a cryptic message: "It's a great day for Literature and for Bob when a Master of its original form is celebrated. Before epic tales and poems were ever written down, they migrated on the winds of the human voice and no voice is greater than Dylan's."[69]

As far back as 2004, Oxford professor and literary critic Christopher Ricks found copious evidence of Dylan's literary qualities. In his study entitled *Dylan's Visions of Sin*, Ricks notes in Dylan's songs theological interpretations connected to the seven deadly sins. He also tracks down the four cardinal virtues—prudence, justice, saneness, and valor—as well as the three heavenly graces: faith, hope, and mercy. Ricks goes on to say that Dylan serves poetry, and he does not hesitate to include the troubadour in his personal pantheon, along

---

67 https://www.rollingstone.com/music/music-features/stephen-king-why-bob-dylan-deserves-the-nobel-prize-105313/

68 https://www.theguardian.com/music/2016/oct/14/leonard-cohen-giving-nobel-to-bob-dylan-like-pinning-medal-on-everest

69 https://www.facebook.com/tomwaits/photos/congrats-from-tom-and-kathleen-to-bob-dylan-on-winning-the-nobel-prize-its-a-gre/10155403404059126/

with Eliot, Samuel Beckett, and various other literary giants of the Anglo-Saxon tradition.[70]

Allow me to mention that the lyrics from the song "Mr. Tambourine Man" are in *The Norton Introduction to Literature*, while the reviews received by Dylan's book *Tarantula*, containing poems and prose, are simply outstanding. Also, regarding *Chronicles: Volume I*, the *New York Times* writes that the work is clear and without temporal linearity, and despite entering into existential labyrinths, it does not lose the thread of the narrative.

As soon as Obama heard of the award, he tweeted, "Congratulations to one of my favorite poets, Bob Dylan, for a well-deserved Nobel." Just four years before Dylan's Nobel win, Obama awarded him the Presidential Medal of Freedom. Established in 1963 by then US president John F. Kennedy, this medal is the highest honor given to civilians and goes to those who have contributed to national and global issues of peace and civilization. Dylan joined such heroes as astronaut John Glenn Jr., former Israeli prime minister Shimon Peres, former US secretary of state Madeleine Albright, and American author Toni Morrison.

Obama said: "These extraordinary honorees . . . challenged us, they've inspired us, and they've made the world a better place."[71]

And last but not least, Billy Collins, one of the most popular American poets, supported Dylan's win by saying, "Dylan's lyrics are in the 2 percent club of songwriters whose lyrics are interesting on the page."[72]

To be considered a candidate for the Nobel Prize, one must be nominated by a member of the Academy, professor of literature, award-winning author, or president of a corresponding artistic association. Dylan's candidacy was discussed as early as 1996, encouraged by his good friend Allen Ginsberg. The Nobel Prize is usually

---

70   https://booksjournal.gr/kritikes/poiisi/3278-einai-o-dylan-poiitis
71   https://sites.ed.gov/whhbcu/files/2011/12/President-Obama-Awards-the-Presidential-Medal-of-Freedom-to-recipient-Toni-Morrison.pdf
72   https://www.svcmusic.org/previous-concert-highlights/the-times-they-are-a-changin-a-dylan-oratorio/

awarded for the overall contribution of an author, and from this point of view, no one can dispute that Dylan's lyrics have influenced many generations. He had been the inspirer of unruly teenagers, bohemian personalities, street intellectuals, and eternal lovers across decades. His fans come from all social strata, from street sweepers to scientists and from cooks to lawyers. His songs appeal to all ages, from schools to nursing homes. Dylan's universal lyrics can be defined as great literature.

Dylan's brilliant songs have been studied and performed in American universities since 1970. When the artistic work of a creator becomes the voice of an entire era or movement, it is perfectly understandable that teachers would want to share the values and virtues found in their work.

Since we are talking about education, let us remember the movie *Dangerous Minds*, which came out in 1995. There is a wonderful scene showing the beautiful and brilliant actress Michelle Pfeiffer, playing the role of the new teacher at a troubled school, reading to the class the lyrics from "Mr. Tambourine Man," and through Dylan's words, she manages to make the students think hard and then understand that poetry is hidden in their souls.

How and who can determine whether a work is high literature? Why shouldn't lyrics set to music belong to the same artistic sphere as poetry? Isn't it absolutely illogical for the lyricist to be considered inferior to the poet?

Let's not forget Ezra Pound,[73] one of the greatest poets of the twentieth century, albeit a controversial one, who wrote cantos—that is, songs. Pound appealed to all the universities of the world to hire singers because he strongly believed that only through melody and rhythm would students feel the heart and soul of poetry.

At this point, I would like to mention some important background. The Academy awarded Dylan as a descendant of a literary

---

73 Read more in the chapter "Ezra Pound."

tradition that began with Homer. In ancient Greece,[74] the epics, choral tragedies, and lyrical poems, like those written by Sappho, were always matched with music. The struggles and adventures of Odysseus are revealed through metered verses, while many rhapsodies are accompanied by a lyre and are sung.

Even in the thirteenth century, "poetry" referred to lyrics and music. Long before Dante's *Divine Comedy*, poetry without meter and melody was unimaginable. Only in the fourteenth century did poetry begin to detach itself from music, though it still retained its oral nature through recitation. For the past three centuries, poetry has been written to be just read, but that is only a short portion of this genre's history. And the auditory aspect of poetry has never truly disappeared. When one writes with measure, one is interested not only in the correct formulation of the words on paper but also in the pleasure and satisfaction of the ears.

In conclusion, I would venture to say that the only difference between musical verse and poetry is the author's intention—whether he writes something to be sung or simply to be read. In my opinion, the sung verse gave birth to poetry as we understand it today. For this reason, lyrics should in no way be considered a subordinate literary genre. I am sure that even the most skeptical people would agree that there are song verses out there that are far more beautiful and poetic than some works labeled high poetry.

Having said that, I wonder if there would be as much backlash about Dylan's award if he declared himself to be a poet and not a musician. Sometimes we humans operate with prejudices and find it difficult to look past our noses. I believe it would be fairer for everyone if the Swedish Academy awarded each literary genre separately—as Hollywood does, for example. I believe that change would motivate and encourage young artists. But to make it happen, some people would have to dig deep in their pockets.

Bob Dylan, with his multidimensional and enigmatic verse, his

---

74 Read more in the chapters "Ancient Greece and Poetry" & "Friedrich Nietzsche."

poetic aura, and his rare performing ability, sometimes reminds me of the Russian writer Anton Chekhov, and at other times, when he plays the role of the prophet, of the visionary poet Arthur Rimbaud.[75] Dylan is unpredictable and versatile. He mixes political and social issues, at times with surrealism and symbolism.[76] He likes to constantly change perspectives, create new identities, and be a few steps ahead of his time. Over the years, he has been troubled by many issues concerning the modern age: war, human rights, environment, religion, politics, death, dreams, hope, travel, and love.

As Astor Piazzolla took the tango—just escaped from the doss-houses of Buenos Aires—and added classical music and jazz to it, turning it into a worldwide sensation, so Dylan has done with his songs. He worked feverishly on folk material and lifted it high. He took blues and country music, processed them, and dressed them in an airy cloak of high poetry and contemplation.

Dylan is a mystic trying to restore within us the lost balance, a marathon runner who shines the light on an ancient tradition that for centuries tried to unite the spirit, the soul, the mind, and the body. With his great poetic songs, he has influenced the collective conscious and unconscious[77] mind and given strength to young artists who may not have the voice and presence of Elvis but who have a soul that brews like a volcano and a mind ready to burst open with ideas that need to be heard. A striking example was left-handed guitar player Jimi Hendrix, who, at the beginning of his career, didn't like to sing at all. But when an album by Bob Dylan dropped into his lap, he changed his mind because he realized that having a great voice was not as necessary to success as passion, honesty, and a truly special way of singing.

I think by awarding Dylan, Stockholm welcomed all great song-writers into its family and now considers them an integral part of

---

75   Read more in the chapter "Arthur Rimbaud."
76   Read more in the chapters "Symbolism in literature" & "Surrealism in literature."
77   Read more in the chapter "Carl Jung."

the world's literary tradition. The year before, the Academy revealed its mood for change and innovation by honoring journalist Svetlana Alexievich[78] with the Nobel Prize in Literature. Her work is more a stitching together of interviews than traditional literature. Also, let's remember the case of Dario Fo,[79] a playwright inspired by the pantomime of the sixteenth-century commedia dell'arte, and the Indian poet Rabindranath Tagore,[80] who wrote beautiful songs. Both won the Nobel Prize in Literature in 1997 and 1913, respectively.

I wonder if the Swedes want to modernize and expand their range by providing access to different social groups. Lately, more awards have been going to women, and Dylan's case suggests an attempt by the Academy to free itself from the label of elitism and to build a different profile—one that is fresher and more accessible to the average person. The Academy may also be bringing to a close the polemic against the literary scene of the United States. In 2008, then secretary of the Academy Horace Engdahl stated that America was an isolated and introverted country that did not translate much foreign literature and did not participate in the global dialogue about the progress and course of art.

In any case, many people will now be focused on how far the Academy is willing to go regarding the expansion of literary boundaries. In closing, let's not ignore that Bob Dylan is a legend of rock music who does not need the validation of a Nobel. Perhaps it is the Academy that urgently needs the light of a shining star.

---

78   Read more in the chapter "Svetlana Alexievich."
79   Read more in the chapters "Dario Fo, Commedia Dell' Arte, and Metalanguage."
80   Read more in the chapter "Rabindranath Tagore."

9

A Little More Discussion

IN 2013, JOHN SUTHERLAND, professor of modern English literature at University College in London, published *A Little History of Literature*. The book received great reviews and was translated into many languages worldwide.

Amazingly, he mentions Dylan's name in two chapters, a fact that was undoubtedly food for discussion in the years leading up to the troubadour's Nobel win. In chapter 17, "Books for You: The Changing Reading Public," he says, "Bestselling poetry is a contradiction in terms, unless we count balladeers such as Bob Dylan and David Bowie."[81]

In chapter 38, "Guilty Pleasures: Best Sellers and Potboilers," he continues:

> The most influential single volume in the history of the form is probably Coleridge and Wordsworth's *Lyrical Ballads*. It helps to unpack the root meanings of those two words. 'Lyrical' goes back to the ancient musical instrument, the lyre—the forerunner of the guitar (Homer is traditionally thought to have recited his epics to lyre accompaniment). 'Ballads' goes back to 'dance' (as does 'ballet'). So, what, then, are Bob Dylan's lyrics, sung to his guitar? What are Michael Jackson's, or Beyoncé's, dance and song videos? What are each new generation's recordings of the ballads of Cole Porter? It's not too outrageous a stretch, for those of an open critical

---

81 Sutherland, John, 2014, *A Little History of Literature*, Yale University Press, Greek Publications-Pataki, p. 167 & 370.

mind, to see as much 'literature' in popular music as there was in that 1802 slim volume by Coleridge and Wordsworth. Put another way, look hard and you'll find pearls in the crud.

Sutherland reminds us that poetry is the poor sister of literature that chronologically precedes any written or printed text, for poetry has more of an oral character. He claims that it is strange to be talking about mass-trade poetry unless it is about Dylan, and he dares elevate his work alongside Homer's epics.

Since we are talking about Greek literature, let's remember the book *Lyrical Art* by Gerasimos Spatalas (1887–1971), a distinguished intellectual and writer who came from the island of the Phaeacians, i.e., today's Corfu.

In the chapter "The Great Art," he writes, "Though poetry and music may seem they have broken up today, they still are two twin sisters who coexist harmoniously. Poetry makes music with words and music makes poetry with sounds. Whoever denies the verse denies the deeper essence of the poem, which is intertwined with the sonic character of the language."[82]

And in the chapter "Lyrically," he continues, "Unfortunately, in recent years younger people have eagerly followed the fashion of writing their poems in arrhythmic and inartistic prose. The acoustical artistic level plummets again to such an extent that almost no distinction is made between artistically sonic verses and constructions."

In other words, poetry and music have been walking hand in hand for centuries, and verse makes up the music of the poem. I believe the above statements, along with all that came before, accurately answer the question of whether Dylan deserved such an honor.

It is also worth mentioning that beyond the written word, there is also theater, a form of high art that deals with physical representation. Ancient tragedy could be considered one of the greatest artistic creations of all time. The works of the original storytellers weren't born

---

82 Spatalas, Gerasimos, 1997, *Lyrical Art*, University of Crete, p. 161 & 276.

to be read. Who even knew how to read six hundred years ago? Before John Gutenberg, people wrote on brittle papyrus, and the only way stories survived was through poems or myths passed down by word of mouth from generation to generation. Back then, the original poet was the minstrel, the traveling soul who sang and played his lute on the streets. His job was to brief the people about the news of the day.

Furthermore, we must not forget that our first experience with stories comes through the voices of our family telling us fairy tales and singing lullabies.

Not only is Bob Dylan a modern rhapsodist who writes metered poetic lines, a singer, and an actor, but he is also a storyteller who loves to tell strange and authentic tales that resonate because he is a Jedi of the American colloquial style. Throughout his fruitful career, Dylan has explored new ways to set distinctive narratives to melody and rhythm in a way unlike any other artist of the rock era.

The Academy doesn't compare Dylan's lyrics to the work of Nobel Prize–winning poets T. S. Eliot, Pablo Neruda, W. B. Yeats, and others. His contribution to literature exists in a separate category. He is a prolific artist with his own style, a hungry reader who loves storytelling as well as wordplay. Just as Sophocles worried about where he would find masks or buskins for his *Antigone*, Dylan wonders if his guitar is tuned before the concert or before a recording.

From my point of view, Dylan approaches his lyrical writing from the same educational background as a "literary" writer. Besides being well read, Dylan has spent most of his life out among artists and everyday folk. And that is the best education anyone can have in this life. Let us remember what Albert Camus said when he won the Nobel in 1957: "Art is a means of stirring the greatest number of people by offering them a privileged picture of common joys and sufferings. It obliges the artist not to keep himself apart; it subjects him to the humblest and the most universal truth."[83]

And Dylan does exactly that. By making us listen to all the

---

83 https://www.nobelprize.org/prizes/literature/1957/camus/speech/

wonders and worries of our world, he stirs us, shakes us up, and makes us contemplate things that truly matter. And that mission is the work of a good artist.

Of course, there are many great poets who have not been shown as much attention as they should have—those who have been wronged, who don't write in an international language, and who only gain recognition after their deaths. But I believe it is only fair that out of the many awards the Academy has given since 1901, at least one should remind us that lyricists—who give us so much joy and spiritual upliftment—belong in the company of great writers. We should feel happy and hopeful; Bob Dylan has shown us that verse addressed to an audience can easily become fire in their hearts and slogans in their mouths.

At the end of the book, you will find a list of all those who have won this prestigious prize. After you have studied the list carefully, I believe you will agree with me that Bob Dylan, an artist who has greatly influenced so many artists and generations, rightfully deserved the Nobel.

~

Bob Dylan is an artist who, throughout his career, has faced harsh criticism. Many times, journalists attacked him, and in my opinion, they unjustly vilified him. Especially after the Newport Festival (1965), when he embraced the electric sound of rock music, he transformed from a folk hero into a Judas-like traitor.

In the film *I'm Not There* (2007), which explores the life of the songwriter, there is a scene where Dylan, annoyed by the irritating and senseless questions of a journalist, writes and sings the surrealistic song "Ballad of a Thin Man," ironically addressing someone named Mr. Jones. I believe he penned these peculiar lyrics to demonstrate that the world of journalism often fails to deeply understand an artist's work.

It's a fact that many journalists do an excellent job, but there are others who simply wish to diminish or even destroy an artist's creation without reason or cause—just because it's in their nature.

Allow me to mention the case of the great Greek composer Manos

Hadjidakis, whom the newspaper *Avriani* ("Tomorrows"), in the 1980s, condemned in the worst way. The things written about him at that time were so disgraceful that I prefer to keep silent about them. For the record, Hadjidakis won the Academy Award for Best Original Song for the film *Never on Sunday* (1960), directed by Jules Dassin, and a little later recorded two amazing albums in America: *Reflections* with the New York Rock & Roll Ensemble, and the orchestral composition *Giaconda's Smile* in collaboration with the unique Quincy Jones.

Certainly, beyond journalists, there are art critics who sometimes unjustly criticize the work and artistic intent of a creator. In the previous chapter, we read some negative critiques regarding Dylan's award, which seemed to lack substance.

At this point, I could provide a series of arguments to support my thoughts on those journalists or art critics who, by writing articles in major newspapers, negatively influence readers and artists' careers. However, as a response, I prefer to quote a scene from the innovative film *Birdman*, directed by Alejandro González Iñárritu. This dark comedy drama won several Oscars: Best Director, Best Picture, and Best Screenplay.

∼

Birdman (2014): The Unexpected Virtue of Ignorance

Former movie superhero Riggan Thomson (Michael Keaton) is struggling to mount an ambitious Broadway adaptation of Raymond's Carver short story "What We Talk About When We Talk About Love."

Riggan hopes that by writing, producing, and acting in this adaptation, he will breathe life into his fragmented self and stagnated career. Riggan wants to prove that he is a real artist and not just a fallen and outdated Hollywood star.

In the following bar scene, Riggan is forced to speak with a critic who has decided to destroy his play.

∼

Movie Scene

Wearing a cream trench coat, Riggan sits at the bar, drinking. He is one of only a few customers. At the other end of the bar sits a woman scribbling on a notepad. In the same bar, a few weeks ago, his colleague Mike (Edward Norton) told him, "You see that woman over there? The one that looks like she just licked a homeless guy's ass? Nothing matters until she writes five hundred words about us in the *New York Times*.... [That's] Tabitha Dickinson. Yes. And believe it or not, the only thing that matters in theater is whether she likes us or not. She does, we run. She doesn't, we're fucked."

Now we see Riggan polish off his drink and ask the bartender for another. While the bartender pours another whiskey for Riggan, a waiter steps up to the bar. The bartender points to a drink. "That's going over to Ms. Dickinson."

At the mention of her name, Riggan tilts his head and looks over at Tabitha. He tells the bartender, "I got it. She's a friend of mine," and tosses a bill onto the bar top.

"Okay," the bartender sings and walks away.

With an air of curiosity, Riggan walks the drink over to the critic, sets it in front of her notebook, and watches her write. She looks up and immediately recognizes him.

Riggan takes a napkin out of his pocket—one that the writer Raymond Carver gave him when Riggan was a young man performing in a play—and sets it on the counter. The napkin reads, THANKS FOR AN HONEST PERFORMANCE.

Riggan points at the napkin. "That was twenty years before I put on that goddammed outfit."

She brushes the napkin to the side. "I don't care."

"I was . . . just . . . you know . . . just before you come tomorrow, I want you—"

"It doesn't matter."

"Okay." Eyes fixed on her, he draws in a deep breath.

"I'm going to destroy your play."

"But you didn't even see it." He smirks and rubs his goatee. "But you know . . . did I do something to offend you?"

"As a matter of fact, you did. You took up space in a theater, which otherwise might have been used on something worthwhile."

Riggan rubs his forehead. "Okay, I mean, you don't even know if it's any good or not . . . I mean."

She turns on her bar stool, looks him dead in the eyes, and says in a low and steady voice, "That's true. I haven't read a word of it or even seen a preview, but after the opening tomorrow, I'm going to turn in the worst review anybody has ever read. And I'm going to close your play. Would you like to know why? Because I hate you. And everyone you represent. Entitled. Selfish. Spoiled. Children. Blissfully untrained, unversed, and unprepared to even attempt real art. Handing each other awards for cartoons and pornography. Measuring your worth in weekends? Well, this is the theater, and you don't get to come in here and pretend you can write, direct, and act in your own propaganda piece without coming through me first. So, break a leg."

Riggan scoffs and, rubbing his goatee, watches the critic go back to her writing. "Wow, what has to happen in a person's life for them to end up becoming a critic, anyway?" He moves closer to her. "What are you writing? Another review, huh? Is it any good? Is it? Did you even see this? Let me read it." He snatches the notepad from her hand.

"I will call the police," she says in an irritated voice.

"No, you won't."

She tries to take the notepad back, but he pulls away, eyes on the notepad, and as he walks behind her, he says in a sarcastic tone, "Callow. Callow is a label." He scrapes his goatee again and stands at the edge of the bar, throwing glances at her. "Lackluster. That's just a label. Margi—" He creases his face. "Marginality. You're kidding me." He huffs again. "Sounds like you need penicillin to clear that up. That's a label too. These are just labels." He half closes his eyes, wrinkles his brow, and in a low voice he says, "You just label everything. That's so fucking laaaazy." He points at her. "You just . . . you're a laaazy fucker. You're a laaaazy . . ." He smirks and picks up a flower from a vase. "You know what this is? You even know what that is?"

With an uninterested expression, she looks him dead in the eyes.

"You don't. You know why? Because you can't see this thing if you don't label it." He taps the flower on her temple. "You must think of all those little noises in your head for true knooowledge."

"Are you finished?"

Tossing the flower at the counter, he says, "No, I'm not finished." He picks up the notepad from the bar and slaps it. "There is nothing in here about technique. There is nothing in here about structure. Nothing in here about intention. It's just a bunch of crappy opinions backed up by even crappier comparisons. You write a couple of paragraphs and . . . you know what. None of this cost you fucking anything." He picks up an empty glass and throws it on the bar top.

To the sound of the shattering glass, Tabitha jolts and watches him hit the air with tight fists. "Nothing, nothing, nothing, nothing." He points at himself and in an emotionally charged voice says, "I'm a fucking actor." He lets out a tense breath. "This play cost me everything. So, I tell you what." He tears a page from her notepad, scribbles on it, brings it in front of her eyes, and says, "You take this fucking malicious, cowardly, shittily written review, and you shove that right the fuck up your wrinkly, tight ass."

They look at each other. Then she gives him a closed-lip smile, nods, and says, "You're no actor. You are a celebrity. Let's be clear on that."

Riggan watches her gather her things. Then she takes the flower from the bar and slides it into his open hand resting on the counter. "I'm gonna kill your play," she says and leaves.

~

In closing, I want to take up another question that ought to concern us. Should we separate the creator from his work?

The list of famous but troubling artists is long. Author Louis-Ferdinand Céline, who wrote the highly entertaining *Journey to the End of the Night*, had many antisemitic opinions, and the famous Charlie Chaplin was accused of being a pedophile. Ezra Pound supported the fascist Benito Mussolini. Would it be right to reject him as an artist and throw his books in the trash because we don't like his cruel and inhumane political ideology? The Greek-born Herbert von Karajan, one of the most famous conductors of all time, became a member of the Nazi Party in 1935. Should we deprive our spirits, hearts, and minds of his music because of this terrible affiliation?

My conclusion is that if an artistic work does not contain a distorted ideology that harms man and nature, then we should judge it objectively as an independent entity. Of course, the ideal is for the work and the creator to go hand in hand, but unfortunately the exact opposite often happens. I guess we must accept that a bunch of bastards have created great art.

But let's go back to Dylan again. Dylan is a distinctive figure who at times has given us fodder for negative comments. But we should always keep in mind that it is only fair to separate the man from his work. And whatever one can find to accuse and judge him on pales in the face of the dark cases of Pound and Karajan.

Let us conclude this one chapter with the statement Neil LaBute—the American playwright, film director, and actor who wrote *In the Company of Men*—made when he heard of the Academy's decision to award Dylan with the Nobel Prize in Literature: "The gods of literature have finally risen from their sleep, yawned and opened their eyes wider than ever before and the results of this awakening smile down on a true and honest creator: Mr. Bob Dylan."[84]

---

84   https://pen.org/should-bob-dylan-have-won-the-nobel-prize-for-literature/

PART THREE

"Suffice it to say, Dylan is a planet to be explored. For a songwriter, Dylan is as essential as a hammer and nails and a saw are to a carpenter. . . . His journey as a songwriter is the stuff of myth because he lives between the ether of his songs."[85]

TOM WAITS

---
[85] https://benjaminjsmith.substack.com/p/dylan-planet

10

I Have a Dream

ON A TRAIN heading to New York City after Martin Luther King's legendary "I Have a Dream" speech, Bob Dylan stumbled upon a newspaper article about William Zantzinger, a White landowner who killed an African American mother, Hattie Carroll, with his cane. William was sentenced to only six months in prison. Outraged by the decision of the court, Dylan immediately wrote "The Lonesome Death of Hattie Carroll." The song was recorded on October 23, 1963. Below we will read about Martin Luther King Jr., and in the following chapter we will read the short story I wrote inspired by Bob Dylan's wonderful lyrics.

∼

In August 1963, 250,000 people gathered in Washington, DC, to protest for civil rights, racial equality, and the right to vote. These same protesters would march that summer in support of a groundbreaking bill that was supposed to end the unequal and horrific treatment of African Americans once and for all. These afflicted people, especially in the Southern states, could not eat in the same restaurants as the Whites, stay in the same hotels, drink from the same taps, buy houses in the same district, or have equal job opportunities.

From the steps of the Lincoln Memorial, Reverend Martin Luther King Jr. delivered the legendary and unforgettable speech "I Have a Dream." In it, King described his dream of freedom and equality arising from a land of slavery and hatred. A year later, he won the

Nobel Peace Prize. This speech has been described as one of the greatest speeches in the English language. John Meacham writes in *Time* magazine, "With a single phrase, King joined Jefferson and Lincoln in the ranks of men who've shaped modern America."[86]

One of the guests was Bob Dylan, who sang "Only a Pawn in Their Game," a song about the assassination of civil rights activist Medgar Evers only two months before.

About a year later, President Lyndon B. Johnson signed the bill into law, a great victory for those who fought, suffered, and were tortured and executed for having a different skin color.

Martin Luther King Jr. was born on January 15, 1929, in Atlanta, Georgia. From the first years of his life, he was exposed to the hatred of the Whites and their inhuman and arrogant behavior. As an adult, he talked about the separating curtains on the trains, which still haunted him. King said, "I was very young when I had my first experience behind the curtain. I felt like a curtain had fallen over my whole life."[87]

At fifteen, King attended Atlanta's Moravian College, a program that accepted gifted students who wanted to become either doctors or lawyers. But in the last year, he dropped out and became a clergyman at the insistence of his father, who was a Baptist priest, receiving a diploma in theology from Crozer in Chester, Pennsylvania, in 1951.

From Crozer, he went to Boston University, where he met his wife, Coretta Scott. There he wrote the thesis *A Comparison of the Conception of God in the Thinking of Paul Tillich and Henry Nelson Wieman*. King believed that God was an active entity and that the salvation of man was found only in faith and love toward the Creator.

After a year as the pastor of a Baptist church in Montgomery, Alabama, and upon the arrest of the seamstress Rosa Parks, who

---

86 https://ukenreport.com/king-the-speech-heard-around-the-world/
87 https://christiannaloupa.wordpress.com/%CE%BC%CE%B1%CF%81%CF%84%CE%B9%CE%BD-%CE%BB%CE%BF%CF%85%CE%B8%CE%B5%CF%81-%CE%BA%CE%B9%CE%BD%CE%B3%CE%BAmartin-luther-king-1929-1968-2/

refused to give up her seat on the bus to a White passenger in early December 1955, King was elected head of the Montgomery Improvement Association, a newly formed protest group. The overworked and downtrodden African Americans gained a man with an amazing ability to speak for them. In his famous speech he said,[88]

> I have a dream that one day this nation will rise up and live out the true meaning of its creed. We hold these truths to be self-evident that all men are created equal. I have a dream that one day out in the red hills of Georgia the sons of former slaves and the sons of former slaveowners will be able to sit down together at the table of brotherhood. I have a dream that one day even the state of Mississippi, a state sweltering with the heat of oppression, will be transformed into an oasis of freedom and justice. I have a dream that my four little children will one day live in a nation where they will not be judged by the color of their skin but by their character. I have a dream today. I have a dream that one day down in Alabama, with its vicious racists, with its governor having his lips dripping with the words of interposition and nullification; that one day right down in Alabama little black boys and black girls will be able to join hands with little white boys and white girls as sisters and brothers. I have a dream today. I have a dream that one day every valley shall be engulfed, every hill shall be exalted, and every mountain shall be made low, the rough places will be made plains and the crooked places will be made straight and the glory of the Lord shall be revealed, and all flesh shall see it together.

A year later, the Black citizens in Montgomery would finally find seats anywhere on the buses.

Always fighting racial discrimination, King created the Southern Christian Leadership Conference (SCLC) of the Southern states, and

---

88 https://www.history.com/topics/black-history/i-have-a-dream-speech

with strong support from the South, he went on tours, gave talks to the people about their political rights, and promoted a political philosophy based on nonviolence.

In November 1967, King and the members of the SCLC gathered to launch the Poor People's Campaign, or Poor People's March, to highlight and find solutions to the problems facing the country's poor. In the spring of 1968, as King was about to go on the Poor People's March to Washington, DC, his tour was interrupted, and instead he went to Memphis, Tennessee, to support a strike by sanitation workers.

While the civil rights movement, the Vietnam War, and the antiwar movement were in full swing, King stood on the second-floor balcony of the Lorraine Motel in Memphis and was shot dead by a White sniper at the age of thirty-nine. His killer, James Earl Ray, a small-time criminal, was in the wind for two months before his arrest. He pled guilty to the shooting and was sentenced to ninety-nine years in prison. He recanted his plea, claiming that he has been framed by a conspiracy, but spent the rest of his life in prison.

Following his death, King was awarded the Presidential Medal of Freedom and the Congressional Gold Medal. After many years, during which various senators, representatives, and the King Center worked to make King's birthday, January 15, a national holiday, the bill to make the first Monday in January Martin Luther King Jr. Day was finally passed in 1983. The first official celebration took place January 20, 1986.

11

The Lonesome Death of Hattie Caroll [89]

"The Lonesome Death of Hattie Caroll" (Lyrics)

William Zantzinger killed poor Hattie Carroll
With a cane that he twirled around his diamond ring finger
At a Baltimore hotel, society gath'rin'
And the cops were called in, and his weapon took from him
As they rode him in custody down to the station
And booked William Zantzinger for first-degree murder
But you who philosophize, disgrace and criticize all fears
Take the rag away from your face, now ain't the time for your tears

William Zantzinger, who at twenty-four years
Owns a tobacco farm of six hundred acres
With rich wealthy parents who provide and protect him
And high office relations in the politics of Maryland
Reacted to his deed with a shrug of his shoulders
And swear words and sneering, and his tongue it was snarling
In a matter of minutes, on bail was out walkin'
But you who philosophize, disgrace and criticize all fears
Take the rag away from your face, now ain't the time for your tears

Hattie Carroll was a maid of the kitchen
She was fifty-one years old and gave birth to ten children
Who carried the dishes and took out the garbage

---

[89] Dylan, Bob, The Lonesome Death of Hattie Carroll, on *The Times They are A-changin'*, Columbia, 1964.

And never sat once at the head of the table
And didn't even talk to the people at the table
Who just cleaned up all the food from the table
And emptied the ashtrays on a whole other level
Got killed by a blow, lay slain by a cane
That sailed through the air and came down through the room
Doomed and determined to destroy all the gentle
And she never done nothing to William Zantzinger
And you who philosophize, disgrace and criticize all fears
Take the rag away from your face, now ain't the time for your tears

In the courtroom of honor, the judge pounded his gavel
To show that all's equal and that the courts are on the level
And that the strings in the books ain't pulled and persuaded
And that even the nobles get properly handled
Once that the cops have chased after and caught 'em
And that the ladder of law has no top and no bottom
Stared at the person who killed for no reason
Who just happened to be feelin' that way without warnin'
And he spoke through his cloak, most deep and distinguished
And handed out strongly for penalty and repentance
William Zantzinger with a six-month sentence
Oh, but you who philosophize, disgrace and criticize all fears
Bury the rag deep in your face for now's the time for your tears.

∽

The Lonesome Death of Hattie Carroll
Short Story by Dimitrios P. Naskos

August 2014. In the far distance, past the flat country, cows graze under a sky splashed in hues of orange, gold, and purple as the red sun sinks on the horizon. A gentle breeze blows the leaves of the fully bloomed cedar tree standing right next to a weather-worn, two-story timber house.

At the back of the house, in the yard, is a Ford F1. It sits on flat tires, its windows are broken, and bales of wheat sit heavy in its bed. Two crows perch on telephone wires. The house is miles outside Austin, Texas. In this part of the state, you get more cows than cars.

A man dressed in dungarees and work boots sits on a rocking chair out front by a window, fondling his cat and gazing at the cows. He has dark skin and gray, limp hair. Next to him lies his dog, King, a German shepherd with his eyes half-closed. With such creatures by his side, neither snake nor rats nor anything of that sort dare come near the property.

From the small radio on the windowsill, Morgan hears the distinctive voice of J. J. Cale singing "Don't Cry, Sister." He takes a sip from his whiskey. *He's gone too,* he thinks. *His heart betrayed him.* And as he strokes Sissy with his rough fingers, a sweet nostalgia washes through him.

I'm turning eighty soon, and it looks like death has lost my tracks, he tells himself. *But I'm fine with that, for I've set a goal to become a centenarian in 2034.* "Don't you agree with me, Sissy?" The cat meows.

Morgan hears the crows cawing and watches them charge toward the sky, where dark clouds have begun to bank up. *I'm sure that if these black birds could speak*, he thinks, *they would only say two words: never again.* He draws in a deep breath, closes his eyes, and hears the scattered raindrops on the roof.

For the past year, since the headstrong Morgan—as his close friend Andrew calls him—fell from the ladder where he had climbed to fix the leaking roof, he's used a cane. "You never listen to me. Now look at your sorry ass," his friend told him in the hospital. And because Morgan's damned rheumatoid arthritis won't leave him alone, he also takes pills to help him sleep.

As for the telephone? At first it rang now and again, but it has been a few months since it stopped ringing. Sometimes, Morgan wonders what it would be like to have a wife and children, desiring not so much to bask in their care but to have someone to talk to and to spend time in their company.

Andrew, usually dressed in cowboy boots, worn-out jeans, and his white cowboy hat and sporting a thick white mustache, lives on a farm a little further away, and he drives over quite often in his van. Sometimes he brings grilled meat with boiled potatoes or roasted chicken with rice. Morgan will make a salad, open a few beers, and after dinner they'll clear the table and play Texas hold 'em. They both love the game, and to make it more interesting, they bet a few dollars. When Morgan wins, Andrew hits his fist on his knee and creases his face. "I can't believe your lucky ass. It's the third time you've picked up pocket aces. Goddamn it." He fixes his ashy gaze on his friend. "Could it be that you cheating me?" he says as Morgan laughs.

Every morning, a teenager in sports socks and shorts, tattoos on his arms and headphones in his ears, halts his electric bike in front of the house and shoves the *Houston Chronicle* in the tilted, rusty mailbox. Then the teenager whistles loudly and speeds off, humming a rap song.

Last night, at eleven o'clock, while Morgan was propped up on pillows in his bed and thumbing through the newspaper in the light of the lamp, he stumbled upon an article about the murder of an African American man, known by family and friends as "the neighborhood peacemaker."

"Let go of me. I can't breathe," cried Eric Garner over and over again as he was being pinned on the ground and locked in a choke hold by a cop who had suspected him of smuggling cigarettes.

Passersby stopped and tried to see what was happening while the shopkeepers came out of their shops with shock in their eyes. They yelled at the cops to let him go. "What are you doing? You will choke him to death! Don't you see he can't breathe!"

Another uniform told them to mind their own business while the unfortunate Eric Garner was breathing his last on that gray ground, in the grip of law, order, and protection.

Morgan let out a heavy sigh, dropped the newspaper atop his worn slippers on the floor, took off his thick-rimmed glasses, and peered out the dark bedroom window for a good while. He was in no mood to read more news; most of the time, it just messed up his head and knotted his stomach. Before switching off the light, he glanced at the dream catcher hanging on the wall above his head and wondered, *How the hell does it catch dreams? And where does it hide them?*

The dream catcher had been given to him by an Indian woman who sat right across from him on the train many years ago. Morgan doesn't remember where he was traveling with his mother during that summery dusk, but he remembers that the Indian woman had straight, sleek, long hair, cherry lips, and hazel-brown eyes.

She had a very strange name. She said they called her Playing with the Deer because she used to spend long hours every day in the meadows, on the slopes, and in the forests. When she noticed Morgan's eyes fixed on the dream catcher around her neck, she took it off and put it around his. Then she stroked his face, smiled at him, and said something in Indian that the little Morgan didn't understand. But he knew that the dream catcher would keep nightmares at bay. And indeed, so far, he can't remember being troubled by them.

Morgan reaches out and turns off the radio. And when he sets his gaze on the drizzle of rain, Hattie Carol's story comes to his mind. The more he thinks about her story, the more tears well up in his eyes. As the years drag by, his love for Hattie grows bigger. And that's because true love never fades with the passing of time. True love is infinite and eternal.

Stroking the cat, Morgan closes his eyes. When the image of

Hattie surfaces, even though fifty years have passed since the last time he saw her, it seems like just yesterday. Here she is, a curvy, good-natured woman who always makes you smile and makes you believe that life is full of colors and pleasant moments. Though Morgan has gone through difficult years, hearing and seeing a lot of bad things, he still can't fathom the idea of her being gone. When he remembers the rich man who hit her on the head with his cane, he feels as if a hand has clenched his heart.

Morgan sighs. *The world is full of madness, envy, and arrogance,* he tells himself. And that is one of the main reasons he has been living far away from people for so many years.

∽

Now his mind travels back to Baltimore, to a February night in 1963. The wind that damned night was so strong it looked likely to uproot the tall trees in the park. John Fitzgerald Kennedy had banned traveling and economic and commercial transactions with Cuba, and just last January, the Viet Cong had achieved their first major victory against the US Army at the Battle of Ap Bac, a small village near Saigon.

Morgan was about thirty years old and six feet tall, with sparkly eyes. He had previously been engaged to his first and last great love, Samantha. They were young and rich with plans. They had decided to marry soon and have many children. "Be patient, baby. Things gonna get better soon. You'll see," he told her while fondling her rich hair sprawled across his muscular chest. But after a while, Samantha moved to Canada with a man who owned his own clothing shops. She rolled out of Morgan's life in a shiny Cadillac and left a folded note under his door that read, PEOPLE CHANGE.

During that time, having an overwhelming desire to create, Morgan was a locomotive on two feet. Since the beginning of the year, he had been hanging around in unemployment offices. He stood in long lines stretching down hallways and outside to the snowy sidewalk and the road. To keep himself warm, he put newspapers under his clothes and inside his boots. "Can I trouble you for a cigarette?" a man with dirty fingernails asked him. He still sees the man's gaunt face clearly in his mind, eyes deep in their sockets, his breaths thick in the air. And Morgan still feels the cold drilling into his bones.

The wheels in his head were turning, and he knew that if given the chance, he could achieve anything. But the person in charge of recruiting gave the jobs to the Whites. He was a tall, stout man, and his face looked as if he were made of wood and his eyes of glass. Morgan sees him coming out of his warm office, standing at the door of the building, and announcing, "Unfortunately, I've got no more jobs for you. Come back tomorrow."

After a month of being cold and hungry, Morgan got lucky. He landed a job as a waiter at Baltimore's old Emerson Hotel, a large building at the intersection of Baltimore and Calvert. Morgan stepped into the shoes of a tall, lanky African American man who went by the name Charlie. Charlie had quit his job because the only thing he cared about was getting back to his studio apartment in the suburbs and blowing his golden saxophone in front of the wardrobe and his hanging clothes. He did that because he believed the sound wouldn't disturb the neighbors that way. Charlie told Morgan he was going to find his artistic fortune in brutally freezing Chicago. "The hell with that fuckin' job. I'm cut for greater things."

One Saturday, a fancy dance was to be held in the central banquet hall adjacent to the lobby of the hotel. The city's high society was invited to the celebration, which was organized by the Club of Retired Officers. That night, Morgan remembers, he was extremely stressed out. How could he not be, considering he had only held a tray two or three times in his life, and that was to help a neighbor who was too ill to work at a restaurant that made all the nearby alleys smell sweet? Morgan gave the money he earned for those days to his neighbor because whenever Morgan was in need, Denzel gave him money and served him a plate of hot food free of charge. "Brother, you stay in bed till you get better," Morgan told him. "And don't you go worrying 'bout nothing. You hear me?"

Friday afternoon before the dance, Morgan went to Emerson to meet with the manager, who was supposed to provide a uniform and explain a few things. The manager, a stocky man with a thin mustache and eyes like small buttons, told him in a stern tone, "You must be polite, never talk back to the guests, and never look White people in the eye. Do you understand?"

Holding the uniform, Morgan walked through the lobby, and as he was about to exit through the revolving door, he heard his name. He turned and saw Hattie Carroll standing in her white apron, smiling brightly at him. "Morgan, baby, what you doin' here?" she asked in surprise. "Been a spell since I saw you last."

She went to him, gazed into his eyes, caressed his face, and gave him a tight, warm hug. At the time, Hattie was fifty-one years old and had ten children from three different marriages.

~

Hattie was born on April 12, 1912, the day the *Titanic* crashed into that cursed iceberg in the Atlantic Ocean. She grew up with Jane, Morgan's mother, in a poor Baltimore neighborhood. They were inseparable friends, together through thick and thin, but one night, a high fever separated them forever. And thus, little Morgan became an orphan, his father having walked out on them when he learned of the pregnancy. Hattie, feeling as though Morgan were her own child, took him in.

Every Sunday, she brought her now eleven children to church to receive Communion and pray. She would open her long and strong arms that looked like wings around her children and sing gospels. "Lord! Lord!" she sang in her angelic voice.

Her third husband was working on the construction of a railroad that would connect Maryland with Ohio. The whole family lived in a semibasement, and when it poured, the apartment flooded. Hattie would rush about the place, wringing towels into buckets. "Don't be afraid, my loves. Now we can bathe with natural water," she told her children, who would perch on the sofa and on the armchairs.

A few months ago, Morgan had run into her on the bus to the city center, close to the market where butchers and greengrocers ran their stores and where you could sit on a bench in the square, look at the statues, and feed the pigeons. When she saw him getting on, she motioned him over. "Morgan, my love, come over here."

Two rows away sat two guys in shiny shoes, suits, trench coats, and hats. They turned, looked at Morgan, and whispered to each other suspiciously. "Don't pay them any mind, my love." Hattie tapped his leg. Then she told him how much she missed his mother and let her brooding gaze wander across the window as the bus rattled through the city.

Morgan still remembers the words she spoke that day: "You know that your mother comes to my dreams, and we talk, we sing, and we laugh when we hang the washing on the terrace or when we cook? Your mother was always worried about you, but it didn't show. She wanted you to succeed in your life and always stay strong. Morgan, my love, don't you ever give up. One day luck will smile at you," she said with tears in her eyes.

∽

So, Saturday night, men in suits, ties, and hats and women in heels, long dresses, and glittering necklaces began to file into the ballroom with an aristocratic air and ample swagger in their movements.

A large chandelier hung from the ceiling, and in each corner sat pots of ferns and palm trees. Lavender-scented candles burned on every table. At the far end of the room, a fire burned majestically in the fireplace.

When Morgan remembers the band that played that night, he cracks a smile and tells his cat, "The Dreamers, that's what they called them: the Dreamers," and he pictures them playing jazz near the wall draped with a burgundy velvet curtain that shimmered in the spotlights hanging from the ceiling.

All the musicians wore black suits and white shirts. The drummer was chubby and wore a hat, and a tall, lanky guy who played the double bass had sunglasses on his angular face. The piano player wore a flat, black hat, and a lit cigarette dangled from his fleshy lips. And the trumpet player was a tall and lean man with high cheekbones, and every time he blew his horn, his cheeks inflated like balloons.

After a short pause, the trumpet player turned to the musicians and said, "Guys, let's play the well-known piece," and the pianist played a strange chord that seemed out of tune. They all smiled and drank whiskey from their glasses. Except for the White drummer, the rest of the musicians were African Americans. At that moment, they started playing their own version of "Summertime (and the Living Is Easy)" by George Gershwin, rocking their bodies to the jazz beat, each musician forming his own distinctive grimaces.

In the kitchen, Morgan wiped the sweat from his neck and forehead with a handkerchief. He was wearing black pants, a white shirt, and a black waistcoat and had loosened his bow tie because he felt like he was suffocating.

"Morgan, my love, don't worry. Think beautiful thoughts, and don't be afraid that you'll drop the tray," Hattie told him and patted his shoulder. "Just imagine you're on a beach somewhere on the West Coast with the woman of your dreams. I'm sure you'll meet her soon." She left the order slip on the aluminum counter and brought her warm palm to his cheek.

Behind the counter stood a cook with a tall white hat on his head, half-buried in steam and wonderful smells. He filled bowls with vegetable soup while two other cooks prepared meat, fish, soufflés, salads, and rice. The waiters were instructed to simply load the trays and serve the customers without speaking to them.

∼

The first time Hattie got married was in 1929, shortly after the stock market crash. In 1933, her husband, Sam, slowly but steadily began to lose his sight from glaucoma until one day he became completely blind.

"Life is not worth living like this," he told Hattie as he sat in an armchair in front of an open window, feeling the spring sun on his face. Hattie tried to soothe him by saying that science was constantly improving, and lately it had started to work wonders.

"Don't stop hoping," she told him and gave him a tight, warm hug.

One afternoon, when she returned to their apartment carrying two bags of food, Hattie felt a strange stillness.

"Sam? You here? Sam?"

After a few agonizing breaths, Hattie dropped the bags on the wooden floor, covered her face with her trembling hands, and lost the ground beneath her feet. She tried to scream but couldn't. The image of her husband with the thick rope around his neck had frozen the blood in her veins. The cops who took him down from the ceiling beam tried to calm her until the ambulance arrived.

Her second husband, Brad, was addicted to gambling and booze. He drank whiskey like a person crossing the Nevada desert on foot drinks water. When the trucking company he worked for fired him, Brad began to roll the dice. He hung out at nefarious places, illegal clubs, and in his thick, pink palms, he shook the dice and threw them on the felt, shouting and making faces, in the hope of winning good money.

Bearded and unkempt, he would stagger back home as the first light broke on the horizon, his breath stinking of booze. He would wake Hattie and ask her, "Baby, gimme a few dollars," and listen to his wife tell him in a sleepy voice, "Brad, cut it out. Let me sleep. I got to work soon. If I lose the job, we're done." A few weeks later, when he laid his hand on their son Tony because the boy said his father's breath turned his stomach, Hattie left him.

Hattie also had a daughter, Julia, who often asked why her twin sister, Kate, couldn't get up from her wheelchair and play with her in the streets where most of the boys in the neighborhood gathered to kick a cloth ball while the girls jumped rope. "Mommy, when will Kate get better? And when will she start to understand when I talk to her? We're seven now," Julia said, her eyes fixed on Kate's bamboo-like legs.

"Soon, my love. I hope very soon," Hattie said, sighing as she ironed.

"Will she be like this forever?" Julia finally asked one day.

"My love, sometimes God tests those he loves the most," Hattie said. She glanced at the wall, at the picture of the Virgin Mary holding baby Jesus in her arms.

∽

At eleven o'clock, Morgan felt a strange tension building as the guests drank, chatted, laughed, and danced to the jazzy vibes.

"Bring me a martini," a retired officer called out to him. The officer wore a tailcoat, and his bald head shone in the light. Morgan nodded and began to collect the empty plates and glasses from the table.

"Bring us two brandies as well," said a lady with a cleavage like Marilyn Monroe's. She held up a hand covered by a pink glove reaching to her elbow and mumbled something in her friend's ear while glancing slyly at a man sitting at the table right across from hers who looked like James Dean.

The band was now in full swing, playing and sweating away. Long fingers went up and down on the double bass, and the cheeks of the horn blower looked like they were going to burst open. The drummer rocked his body, and the pianist tapped his shiny shoe to the rhythm and played the piano skillfully with his dexterous fingers.

Morgan came back out of the kitchen sweating and sick to his stomach. He stood by the band and scanned the room, his gaze reeled in by a painting of Abraham Lincoln, who seemed to be staring into the future with certainty. Morgan told himself, *The musicians are lucky because they can feel free as birds.*

"Hey, you!" a skinny guy with a hooked nose snapped. "Where's your mind?"

"Sorry, sir," Morgan said and moved over to the table, picking up the empty glasses as the man gave his order and drew on his fat cigar.

About ten minutes before the pendulum of the wall clock struck midnight, a man entered the room. He had on a white suit and a top hat. He held a cheap toy cane, three gold rings shone on his fingers, and his face was powdered white. He was a husky six foot one and stood at the edge of the room, his red eyes betraying lack of sleep. Cigarette smoke hovered around him. Coughing, he pulled a purple handkerchief from his vest with the initials "W. Z." embroidered on it.

After wiping his mouth and the sweat from his forehead, he swaggered toward the bar at the other end of the room. By the time he got there, he had bumped into two guys, cursed, and shoved a waiter, who luckily wasn't holding a full tray.

"Get out of my face, you nigger!" he said and clenched his fist. "Get out of my face before I throw you in the Mississippi River."

At the bar, he drew up a stool and let his snake eyes skim over the bottles standing on the shelves. "You, pour me a bourbon," he told Hattie, who a few minutes ago had stepped into Pete's shoes while the bartender went on a break.

∼

William Zantzinger was twenty-four years old and the only son of a family that owned a vast tobacco plantation. He lived with his parents in a colonnaded mansion with a pool, several servants milling about, and many expensive cars parked in front. Quite often, helicopters would land at the edge of the estate, carrying famous businessmen and politicians. His father, Michael, a bald and bearded man who had lost his left arm in a motorcycle racing accident, got sloshed on bourbon all day, flirted with the maids, and disregarded state laws.

His mother, Ariel, a tall blond woman who constantly pursed her lips and rolled her eyes in exasperation as though everything were going south, came from a family with ties to the Ku Klux Klan. When African American children started attending the same schools as the White children about a decade earlier, the hooded men caused—in Little Rock, the capital of Arkansas—serious bloodshed, forcing Eisenhower to send in paratroopers and the National Guard to control the situation. "Just look at how they spread around us, like ants," she used to say. "In no time at all, they'll outnumber us."

The Cold War was now at its height, and the battle for the conquest of space was on the front pages of the newspapers.

"You think another world war will break out?" his cousin had asked the other day as William drove his convertible.

"If the Communists dare come over to our country, they will regret it bitterly," William said, and with the wind in his blond hair, he brandished a gun that shone in the moonlight.

"Bravo, William!" his cousin cried boisterously.

"Matt, there are two things I hate the most. Russian ruts and niggers." William laughed out loud.

~

Now William was staring at Hattie as she poured drinks.

"Hey, didn't you hear what I said? Pour me a bourbon." His voice was strict and strong.

Hattie looked at him and said with a smile, "Sir, I'll be with you in a minute," then sang in a low voice, "Southern trees bear a strange fruit, blood on the leaves and blood at the root"—the opening lyrics from Billie Holiday's song "Strange Fruit," which the band had just begun to play. The song was about the lynching of Blacks in America.

William's gaze turned violent. "Didn't you hear what I told you?" He gritted his teeth. "Bourbon. Now!" He banged the bar top. Though Hattie heard the hatred in his voice and saw it in his eyes, she merely nodded and smiled again. A few guests turned and stared at him.

In the last two days, he had been drinking in the streets and alleyways of Baltimore until dawn. He ended up in Emerson by chance—or rather, because fate wanted him to be here. Passing the hotel, he found his attention drawn by the music.

With his elbows on the bar, his gaze grew wilder as he snorted through his nose like a raging bull. "Negro, bourbon now!" He slammed the bar with his fist again.

A middle-aged White man told him not to shout or curse at Hattie. But William didn't pay him any mind. Hattie gazed into his powdered face and asked him to wait half a minute.

All at once, William pushed the stool to the floor, grasped his cane, and stretched, cursing, over the bar, bashing Hattie on the head with all his might. All the while, people were dancing, waiters were coming and going, and a stocky, smiling official at the door was shaking hands with a senator.

A man rushed at William and punched him hard in the chin. Losing his balance, William managed to grab the edge of the bar to break his fall. Another man yanked the cane from his hand while a third ran to the front desk to call the police.

A few minutes later, Hattie was sitting in a chair by the refrigerators in the kitchen, holding her head. She felt dizzy and sick to her stomach.

"Baby, what happened?" Pete, the bearded barman, asked. "You okay?"

"I feel kinda weird," she said. She was seeing spots of light. By the time Pete came back with a glass of water, Hattie had collapsed to the floor and passed out.

Morgan was busy helping Amanda with the coat check. As he handed out coats to the guests, he saw cops rush into the ballroom and then emerge gripping William's arms. The band had stopped playing, and the hubbub of the guests hovered in the space. By the time Morgan realized what had happened, the paramedics were carrying Hattie out on a stretcher. Her eyes were closed. Morgan's heart sank.

The next day, when he heard that Hattie had died of cerebral hemorrhage, he quit his job and spent a long stretch of time alone and isolated. He couldn't believe that Hattie was dead. To make ends meet in the aftermath, Morgan worked odd jobs.

Half a year later, in August, he read that William Zantzinger had been charged with manslaughter but was sentenced to only six months in prison. As the convicted man descended the steps of the courthouse in handcuffs, he said, "I'll just miss a lot of snow" and smiled at the reporters and photographers.

That hot afternoon, the distraught Morgan walked up a slope bordering the Baltimore cemetery and looked at the gray sky and the birds flying low. Then he looked down at the cypress trees circling the cemetery and spotted two crows sitting on a wire.

"Never again," Morgan said. "Never again." Tears streamed down his sad face.

〜

Though half a century has passed since that cursed night, Morgan still feels her soft touch and her warm embrace, and he remembers when Martin Luther King raised his hand to the crowd and shouted, "I have a dream!"

As for that rich man, Morgan doesn't care. He heard rumors that William was torn to pieces by a crocodile in Vietnam. Once upon a time, if you asked Morgan whether he wanted revenge or not, he would have said yes, but he's not sure anymore. Blaming William is too easy. *Maybe we should all sit down and think about the real reasons behind racial prejudice and how we can destroy this unjust, unethical, and inhumane system once and for all.* Morgan thinks William was just a pawn on the chessboard or a victim with a twisted mind.

When will people understand that what unites them is far more important and numerous than the things that separate them? Morgan wonders. *When will compassion and love wipe away all traces of envy and hate?*

The rain has stopped, and in the sky, you can see countless stars.

Sissy is gone, having dashed out of Morgan's lap a while ago, rushing to the backside of the house to catch a daring four-legged intruder.

Now Morgan stands on the veranda with one hand in the pocket of his dungarees and the other holding a half-full glass of whiskey. As soon as King sits next to him, he gives the loyal dog a treat, pats him on the head, and says, "My good friend. Many moons ago, I had me many dreams." Nodding, he drinks a mouthful of whiskey.

Yes, he once dreamed that when he became old, he would have many grandchildren who would play in his yard and fill the air with happy voices and laughter. To this day, he doesn't really know what went wrong. Maybe it was the betrayal of his great love, Samantha. Many women came and went in his life after that, but nothing came of it. Maybe deep down he didn't want to have children and raise them in this rotten place. Or maybe it just wasn't meant to happen. *Yes, that's probably the reason. It wasn't meant to happen.* At least, that's what he wants to believe.

Morgan heads down the front stoop and, dragging his feet, stands in the middle of the yard. King follows him in silence. Morgan looks at the horizon, and then his gaze climbs the sky to where the brightest of all stars, Aposperitis, shines eternally. She is Aphrodite, the goddess of beauty. With his nostalgic gaze fixed on that bright star, Morgan whispers, "Hello, Hattie."

EPILOGUE

BOB DYLAN CAME to Greece four times: to the National Stadium of Patra and the Panathenaic Stadium in 1989; the Lycabettus Theater of Athens in 1993; the Terra Vibe Park of Attica in 2010; and the Port of Thessaloniki and the Terra Vibe Park of Attica in June 2014.

The day Dylan played in Thessaloniki, I sat in the first row, pleased to be alongside a friend of mine, a member of the organizing committee. In the background, the sun sank into the horizon, and sailboats with their billowing sails crossed the Thermaikos bay under pink and orange hues. At the edge of the harbor, huge cranes stood motionless as seagulls flew low over the sea, eyes alert, beaks at the ready.

The place was so crammed with people that latecomers couldn't find an empty spot to stand in. Most of the audience sat in chairs, but many stood drinking beer from cans. Right across from where I sat stretched the big stage, covered with guitars, pianos, drums, consoles, and microphones. We all eagerly awaited a close look at the guy wearing shiny gloves and a cowboy hat.

As the day faded and the moon appeared behind the mountain of Hortiatis, Bob Dylan came on stage and immediately began strumming the guitar and singing "Things Have Changed." Within the next two hours, we listened to various songs: "Tangled Up in Blue," "Love Sick," "High Water (For Charley Patton)," "Simple Twist of Fate," "Forgetful Heart," "Summer Days," "A Hard Rain's A-Gonna Fall," "Long And Wasted Years," "All Along the Watchtower," and "Blowin' in the Wind."

Dylan chose a repertoire based mainly on his latest records with some references to some of his classic moments, which he changed melodically. Except for a bow at the end of the concert, he did not communicate with the audience at all, which drew negative reactions.

In the following days, some journalists called him indecent and the evening boring, as it ended at eleven without including any songs reminiscent of the old rock era and Dylan did nothing to create a pleasant and fun atmosphere.

But Bob Dylan is not a performer who flatters his audience. Evidently, he often doesn't play the songs people love from the sixties and the seventies, perhaps because he cannot support them, either interpretively or ideologically. He has grown and evolved as a man and as an artist. He has changed, and he always wants to be honest with himself and with the people paying to hear him perform. He chooses what to sing depending on the period and the season, singing whatever he is interested in, whatever revives him and makes him feel good. At least, that's what I think.

When I saw him on stage, he was veiled with something metaphysical and transcendent from glorified times of the past. When he sings, he masquerades as an actor playing different roles but keeps his identity and his essence intact. I feel he knows himself from the bottom of his soul, and he is without a shadow of a doubt the man who brought rock music closer to great literature. I would say that he is a free artist who alternately rejects and accepts politics, fashion, and propriety as easily as he changes the strings on his guitar.

Dylan is known to steer clear of nostalgia and anything that keeps him anchored in the past. His gaze is always fixed on the horizon, as if whispering to us that "times are changing." Sometimes backward.

Every time I hear, "How many deaths will it take till he knows that too many people have died?" for some strange reason, it brings to mind the Seikilos epitaph.

The Greek man Seikilos, who lived around 200 BC in Tralles in Asia Minor, is known for creating the world's most ancient surviving song. He wrote the poem on a forty-centimeter-high cylindrical column, an inscription in Greek words accompanied by music punctuation marks that defined the melodic line of his composition. He created it to honor his wife, Evterpi.

At the top of the column, his name is written, as well as the intent of the song: ΕΙΚΩΝ Η ΛΙΘΟΣ ΕΙΜΙ. ΤΙΘΗΣΙ ΜΕ ΣΕΙΚΙΛΟΣ ΕΝΘΑ ΜΝΗΜΗΣ ΑΘΑΝΑΤΟΥ ΣΗΜΑ ΠΟΛΥΧΡΟΝΙΟΝ. Translation: "I the stone am one picture. Seikilos put me here as a timeless mark of eternal memory."

Then the verses follow with the melodic symbols: ΟΣΟΝ ΖΗΣ ΦΑΙΝΟΥ, ΜΗΔΕΝ ΟΛΩΣ ΣΥ ΛΥΠΟΥ. ΠΡΟΣ ΟΛΙΓΟΝ ΕΣΤΙ ΤΟ ΖΗΝ, ΤΟ ΤΕΛΟΣ Ο ΧΡΟΝΟΣ ΑΠΑΙΤΕΙ. Translation: "As long as you live make sure you shine, don't be sorry at all. For a while life lasts, time demands its payment."

I feel like Bob Dylan, through "Blowin' in the Wind," is speaking to the first troubadour in the world, telling Seikilos he would like to meet him. And I am certain that Seikilos never stopped singing throughout the centuries about love. He might be off teaching melodies to the animals in the forest.

I have often wondered what the point of art is if it doesn't help you realize that you are just a passerby in this life. Some of us are tourists; others are travelers. What is the essence of life if you can't fill your soul with light? Why do we feel the need to speak, sing, and express ourselves after looking at the high mountains, the vast seas, and the starry skies? Why do we take walks in the spring gardens, on the plains, and on the slopes of the mountains if we do not wish to become one with the unsolved and inexplicable enigma of our existence?

> Our words are the children of many people.
> They are sown, they are born like infants.
> They take root and nourish with blood.
> As the pines hold the form of the air,
> while the air is gone, it's not there.
> The words themselves, guard the form of Man,
> and the man is gone, he is not there.
>
> GEORGE SEFERIS
> Nobel Prize in Literature, 1963

DIONYSIS SAVVOPOULOS

THIS TALL SONGWRITER was born in Thessaloniki in December 1944. In my opinion, he is the most important Greek songwriter maintaining the tradition of the troubadour. He writes metered verses that are considered high poetry, then sets them to music and sings them accompanied by his guitar. His voice is charismatic, and every concert resembles a theatrical performance.

Savvopoulos made me love Bob Dylan even more. In 1997, the album *The Hotel* was released in the Greek market and included arrangements of Lou Reed's "Perfect Day," Nick Cave's "Into My Arms," Jethro Tull's "Too Old to Rock 'n Roll," etc. Among these songs you can find two of Dylan's: "All Along the Watchtower" and "The Wicked Messenger." The first time I heard them on the radio, I was a high school student. I got so excited.

Over the years I delved deeper into the work of the Greek troubadour, and little by little, I discovered great, dynamic songs, such as "The Birds of Misfortune," "I Once Saw Anna," "The Lost Children," "Ode to Georgios Karaiskakis," "Ballos," "The Demosthenes Lexis," "Black Sea," "The Deadly Loneliness of Alexis Aslanis," "Planes and Steamships," "Long Zeibekiko for Nikos," and "Damned Greeks."

Savvopoulos combined wonderful pieces and colors from the vast canvas of art, creating unprecedented, original material that moved and influenced generations in Greece. It didn't take me long to realize that this musical and poetic wealth had spread its web all the way to American folk rock.

In 2011, Savvopoulos released four illustrated booklets related to ancient Greek mythology. Each one was accompanied by a CD of songs. I still remember how impressed I was. This was a project that concerned the young and old alike, because the lyrics carry the warmth of spoken word and the joy of the narration, combining the magic of fairy tales with the wonder of the imagination and a dreamy journey through time.

In 2013, when the global economic crisis covered the sky like a threatening cloud, Savvopoulos decided to translate, direct, and perform onstage the famous *Wealth* by Aristophanes. This timeless work scorches people's obsession with hoarding money and material wealth. I especially liked the moment when Savvopoulos presented Poverty—or if you prefer, Austerity—to explain that happiness is not hidden in a chest filled with rubies, diamonds, and gold but rather in the infinite treasures of the soul.

In November 2017, the Aristotle University of Thessaloniki awarded Dionysis Savvopoulos an honorary doctorate from the Department of Philology, recognizing in this way his enormous contribution to the field of Greek music and poetry.

Now let us read what Savvopoulos told the Greek music magazine *Metronomos* about Bob Dylan:[90]

> What Dylan did was very important. He set poetry to the American folk song and turned it more profound. He was the first poet in the pop industry. Bob Dylan's songs and lyrics have long been a part of daily life for millions of people all around the world. At this moment, the Nobel award is of utmost importance. Globalization, the economic crisis, terrorism, immigration, and the rise of semi-savage political formations inject fear into the souls of people, who gravely turn to their roots, where the need for survival prevails over brutality, but also the light of the rhapsodes, Homer and the lyric poets. By honoring Bob Dylan, a leading artist, with the Nobel Prize, I feel that the Swedish Academy wants to keep that light burning still.

---

90 https://www.mousikaproastia.gr/2022/01/bob-dylan.html

ACKNOWLEDGMENTS

MANY THANKS TO my close friend Georgios Andritsos for the literary editing of the Greek text and its translation into the English language and for initiating me into the world of creative writing; to the tireless and positive Sofia Verginis for the grammatical and syntactic work; to Manolis Deligiannakis and Notis Katselis for their contribution to the final structure of the book; to my publisher John Koehler for his trust, and to Hannah Woodlan for the American editing; to Sister Miranda Chrysomallis for the ideas and the inspirations that came after endless discussions and fights; and last but not least, I thank Father Petros—without him, everything would have been different.

Of course, I thank my wife, Anastasia Theodorakopoulos, who is always by my side and supports me. Her love is a light in the dark night.

BACK PAGES

I was at Glastonbury. Do you know my Bob Dylan story? Well. I was at Glastonbury which is this festival thing, and there's a sort of a formation of trailers where the bands stay, and they're in a square, and it always rains at Glastonbury, it just always rains, and it rained a lot and there was a lot of mud. This is a very important part of it. A lot of mud and water and grossness in between the trailers. And I walked out of my trailer, I was having a cigarette when a trailer door opened across the other side of the mud, and this guy walks out with a hoodie on. You know one of those? A hoodie. So, what you call it? I don't know I never worn one. And he just starts walking through the mud toward me, and I start panicking because I think it's like someone . . . a roadie or something like that, wants to come and have a conversation or something like that, anyway he gets there, and this little cold frail hand comes out of his sleeve, shakes me and I look at him, and it's Bob Dylan. He goes "I like what you do" and I'm like "I like what you do too," and then there was this terrible silence, and he just turned and walked back, and it's one of those moments, maybe we've all had them when you just . . . there was so much to ask and I didn't, but it's one of those moments that can't be really taken away.[91]

Nick Cave

---

[91] https://faroutmagazine.co.uk/nick-cave-first-meeting-with-bob-dylan/

A SELECTION OF LYRICS

"Masters of War" (Lyrics)[92]

Come you masters of war
You that build the big guns
You that build the death planes
You that build all the bombs
You that hide behind walls
You that hide behind desks
I just want you to know
I can see through your masks

You that never done nothin'
But build to destroy
You play with my world
Like it's your little toy
You put a gun in my hand
And you hide from my eyes
And you turn and run farther
When the fast bullets fly

Like Judas of old
You lie and deceive
A world war can be won
You want me to believe
But I see through your eyes
And I see through your brain
Like I see through the water

---

[92] Dylan, Bob, Masters of War, on *The Freewheelin' Bob Dylan*, Columbia, 1963.

That runs down my drain

You fasten all the triggers
For the others to fire
Then you sit back and watch
While the death count gets higher
You hide in your mansion
While the young peoples' blood
Flows out of their bodies
And is buried in the mud

You've thrown the worst fear
That can ever be hurled
Fear to bring children
Into the world
For threatenin' my baby
Unborn and unnamed
You ain't worth the blood
That runs in your veins

How much do I know
To talk out of turn?
You might say that I'm young
You might say I'm unlearned
But there's one thing I know
Though I'm younger than you
That even Jesus would never
Forgive what you do

Let me ask you one question
Is your money that good?
Will it buy you forgiveness?
Do you think that it could?
I think you will find
When your death takes its toll

All the money you made
Will never buy back your soul

And I hope that you die
And your death will come soon
I'll follow your casket
On a pale afternoon
I'll watch while you're lowered
Down to your deathbed
And I'll stand o'er your grave
'Til I'm sure that you're dead

"Only a Pawn in Their Game" (Lyrics)[93]

A bullet from the back of a bush took Medgar Evers' blood
A finger fired the trigger to his name
A handle hid out in the dark
A hand set the spark
Two eyes took the aim
Behind a man's brain
But he can't be blamed
He's only a pawn in their game

A South politician preaches to the poor white man
"You got more than the blacks, don't complain
You're better than them, you been born with white skin," they explain
And the Negro's name
Is used, it is plain
For the politician's gain
As he rises to fame
And the poor white remains
On the caboose of the train
But it ain't him to blame
He's only a pawn in their game

The deputy sheriffs, the soldiers, the governors get paid
And the marshals and cops get the same
But the poor white man's used in the hands of them all like a tool
He's taught in his school
From the start by the rule
That the laws are with him
To protect his white skin
To keep up his hate

---

93 Dylan, Bob, Only a Pawn in Their Game, on *The Times They Are a-Changin'*, Columbia, 1964.

So he never thinks straight
'Bout the shape that he's in
But it ain't him to blame
He's only a pawn in their game

From the poverty shacks he looks from the cracks to the tracks
And the hoof beats pound in his brain
And he's taught how to walk in a pack
Shoot in the back
With his fist in a clinch
To hang and to lynch
To hide 'neath the hood
To kill with no pain
Like a dog on a chain
He ain't got no name
But it ain't him to blame
He's only a pawn in their game

Today Medgar Evers was buried from the bullet he caught
They lowered him down as a king
But when the shadowy sun sets on the one
That fired the gun
You'll see by his grave
On the stone that remains
Carved next to his name
His epitaph plain
"Only a pawn in their game"

"Hurricane" (Lyrics)[94]

Pistol shots ring out in the barroom night
Enter Patty Valentine from the upper hall
She sees a bartender in a pool of blood
Cries out, "My God, they killed them all"

Here comes the story of the Hurricane
The man the authorities came to blame
For somethin' that he never done
Put in a prison cell, but one time he could-a been
The champion of the world

Three bodies lyin' there, does Patty see
And another man named Bello, movin' around mysteriously
"I didn't do it" he says, and he throws up his hands
"I was only robbin' the register, I hope you understand"

"I saw them leavin'," he says, and he stops
"One of us had better call up the cops"
And so Patty calls the cops
And they arrive on the scene
With their red lights flashin' in a hot New Jersey night

Meanwhile, far away in another part of town
Rubin Carter and a couple of friends are drivin' around
Number one contender for the middleweight crown
Had no idea what kinda shit was about to go down

When a cop pulled him over to the side of the road
Just like the time before and the time before that
In Paterson that's just the way things go
If you're black you might as well not show up on the street
'Less you want to draw the heat

---

94   Dylan, Bob, Hurricane, on *Desire*, Columbia, 1976.

Alfred Bello had a partner and he had a rap for the cops
Him and Arthur Dexter Bradley were just out prowlin' around
He said, "I saw two men runnin' out, they looked like middleweights
Jumped into a white car with out-of-state plates"
And Miss Patty Valentine just nodded her head
Cop said, "Wait a minute, boys, this one's not dead"
So they took him to the infirmary
And though this man could hardly see
They told him he could identify the guilty men

Four in the mornin' and they haul Rubin in
They took him to the hospital and they brought him upstairs
The wounded man looks up through his one dyin' eye
Says, "Why'd you bring him in here for? He ain't the guy!"

Here's the story of the Hurricane
The man the authorities came to blame
For somethin' that he never done
Put in a prison cell, but one time he could-a been
The champion of the world

Four months later, the ghettos are in flame
Rubin's in South America, fightin' for his name
While Arthur Dexter Bradley's still in the robbery game
And the cops are puttin' the screws to him, lookin' for somebody to blame

"Remember that murder that happened in a bar?"
"Remember you said you saw the getaway car?"
"You think you'd like to play ball with the law?"
"Think it mighta been that fighter that you saw runnin' that night?"
"Don't forget that you are white"

Arthur Dexter Bradley said "I'm really not sure"
The cops said, "A poor boy like you, could use this break
We got you for the motel job and we're talkin' to your friend Bello
You don't want to have to go back to jail, be a nice fellow
You'll be doin' society a favor
That son of a bitch is brave and gettin' braver
We want to put his ass in stir
We want to pin this triple murder on him
He ain't no Gentleman Jim"

Rubin could take a man out with just one punch
But he never did like to talk about it all that much
"It's my work," he'd say, "and I do it for pay
And when it's over I'd just as soon go on my way"

Up to some paradise
Where the trout streams flow and the air is nice
And ride a horse along a trail
But then they took him to the jailhouse
Where they try to turn a man into a mouse

All of Rubin's cards were marked in advance
The trial was a pig-circus, he never had a chance
The judge made Rubin's witnesses drunkards from the slums
To the white folks who watched, he was a revolutionary bum

And for the black folks he was just a crazy nigger
No one doubted that he pulled the trigger
And though they could not produce the gun
The D.A. said he was the one who did the deed
And the all-white jury agreed

Rubin Carter was falsely tried
The crime was murder one, guess who testified?
Bello and Bradley and they both baldly lied

And the newspapers, they all went along for the ride
How can the life of such a man
Be in the palm of some fool's hand?
To see him obviously framed
Couldn't help but make me feel ashamed to live in a land
Where justice is a game

Now all the criminals in their coats and their ties
Are free to drink martinis and watch the sun rise
While Rubin sits like Buddha in a ten-foot cell
An innocent man in a living hell

Yes, that's the story of the Hurricane
But it won't be over till they clear his name
And give him back the time he's done
Put in a prison cell, but one time he could-a been
The champion of the world

DISCOGRAPHY

2020—*Rough and Rowdy Ways*
2017—*Triplicate*
2016—*Fallen Angels*
2015—*Shadows in the Night*
2012—*Tempest*
2009—*Christmas in the Heart*
2009—*Together through Life*
2006—*Modern Times*
2001—*"Love and Theft"*
1997—*Time Out of Mind*
1993—*World Gone Wrong*
1992—*Good as I Been to You*
1990—*Under the Red Sky*
1989—*Oh Mercy*
1988—*Down in the Groove*
1986—*Knocked Out Loaded*
1985—*Empire Burlesque*
1983—*Infidels*
1981—*Shot of Love*
1980—*Saved*
1979—*Slow Train Coming*
1978—*Street Legal*
1976—*Desire*
1975—*The Basement Tapes*
1975—*Blood on the Tracks*

1974—*Planet Waves*
1973—*Dylan*
1973—*Pat Garrett and Billy the Kid*
1970—*New Morning*
1970—*Self Portrait*
1969—*Nashville Skyline*
1967—*John Wesley Harding*
1966—*Blonde on Blonde*
1965—*Highway 61 Revisited*
1965—*Bringing It All Back Home*
1964—*Another Side of Bob Dylan*
1964—*The Times They Are A-Changin'*
1963—*The Freewheelin' Bob Dylan*
1962—*Bob Dylan*

PANORAMIC VIEW: TIMETABLE

THIS PANORAMIC VIEW begins from the moment Bob Dylan was born and stretches through today. We can observe the songwriter's creative journey alongside certain significant historical, scientific, and musical events.

Date	Bob Dylan	History	Science	Music
1941	Dylan is born in Minnesota.	Japan attacks Pearl Harbor		
1957	As a student, Dylan joins a teenage band, Golden Chords.		The Soviet Union launches Sputnik 1.	
1959	Dylan goes to college, but along the way, he drops out and begins to listen and sing at different venues.			Rock and roll has become a global frenzy, initiated by Bill Haley's success in 1955.
1961 1962	Dylan signs with Columbia Records to produce his first album.	The Soviet Union sends missiles to Cuba.	Yuri Gagarin travels to space.	
1963	Dylan releases his second album, which contains the hymn "Blowin' in the Wind."	Martin Luther King Jr. delivers his iconic speech, "I Have a Dream."		The Beatles are on the rise.
1964	Dylan comes out with a protest album: *The Times They Are A-Changin'*.	Following the assassination of Kennedy, Lyndon Johnson becomes the president of the United States.		The Animals arrange "The House of the Rising Sun."

Date	Bob Dylan	History	Science	Music
1965 1966	Dylan begins to play electric guitar and releases the albums *Bring It All Back Home*, *Highway 61 Revisited*, and *Blonde on Blonde*.	American soldiers are shipped over to Vietnam.		
1967	Dylan goes back to playing folk, and *John Wesley Harding* is released.	Ernesto Che Guevara is assassinated in Bolivia.		The hippies coin "Summer of Love."
1968 1969	*Nashville Skyline* is released, where Dylan sings in a different voice.	Civil unrest breaks out throughout France and lasts several weeks.	Neil Armstrong walks on the moon.	The Woodstock music festival is organized.
1970	The album *New Morning* hits the market.			The Beatles break up.
1971	The experimental prose and poetry collection *Tarantula* is published.			Jim Morrison dies in a bathtub in Paris, France.
1972	Dylan accepts a role in the movie *Pat Garret and Billy the Kid*. He also composes the film's soundtrack.	The Watergate scandal breaks out.	The Dutch company Phillips releases the videotape on the market.	
1973 1974	Dylan releases the album *Planet Waves*, which contains "Forever Young," and he goes on tour with the Band.	A chess match between two men, an American and a Russian, takes on a political dimension during the Cold War.		The band Pink Floyd releases the amazing album *The Dark Side of the Moon*.
1975	The successful tour Rolling Thunder Revue gets on the road.		Bill Gates sets up Microsoft.	

Date	Bob Dylan	History	Science	Music
1976 1977	Dylan writes the famous "Hurricane," which tells us about the unfair incarceration of the boxer Rubin Carter.		Steve Jobs sets up Apple.	Elvis Presley passes away.
1979	Dylan turns to Christianity.	Margaret Thatcher becomes the first female prime minister of the UK.	The Walkman hits the market.	Pink Floyd completes the album *The Wall*.
1980	The album *Saved* enters circulation, with songs influenced by spirituals and gospels.			John Lennon is assassinated.
1985	Dylan participates in a charity single: "We Are the World."	Mikhail Gorbachev announces perestroika.		Two historically important concerts, Live Aid, are organized in Philadelphia and London.
1988 1989	Dylan helps form the Traveling Wilburys.	The Berlin Wall comes down.	The WWW (World Wide Web) begins development.	Madonna becomes the top pop idol.
1990 1991	Dylan releases two albums, *Oh Mercy*, with its infamous "Political World," and *Under the Red Sky*.	The Gulf War breaks out, and the Soviet Union collapses.		Freddy Mercury passes away from AIDS.
1993 1994	*World Gone Wrong* comes out.	Apartheid finally comes to an end.		Kurt Cobain commits suicide.
1997	Dylan releases *Time Out of Mind* and wins a Grammy.		IBM's computer beats Russian grandmaster Garry Kasparov in a game of chess.	

Date	Bob Dylan	History	Science	Music
2000	Dylan wins an Oscar for the song "Things Have Changed."			
2001	Dylan comes out with the prophetic album *"Love and Theft."*	After a terrorist attack, the Twin Towers collapse in New York City.		The musician John Phillips, who composed "San Francisco," an anthem dedicated to hippies, passes away.
2004 2006	The album *Modern Times* comes out, with prescient hints about the coming economic crisis.	Hurricane Katrina devastates New Orleans.	Facebook is launched.	
2008 2010	Dylan releases *Christmas in the Heart* and, to shoot the music video, slips into a Santa costume.	The global financial service Lehman Brothers collapses.		The king of pop, Michael Jackson, passes away.
2012 2015	The album *Shadows in the Night* is released with adaptations of Frank Sinatra's songs.		CERN claims to have discovered the God particle.	
2016	Bob Dylan wins the Nobel Prize in Literature.			Leonard Cohen passes away.
2020	Dylan launches the handcrafted collection Heaven's Door whiskey.		Stephen Hawking passes away.	

Detailed Timeline of History, Science, and Music (1941–2020)

- In December 1941, a swarm of Japanese Mitsubishi A6M Zeros swoop down on the US base at Pearl Harbor, dropping bombs and causing great destruction and death. Right away, America abandons its isolationist policy and prepares to fight Germany, Italy, and Japan, known as the Axis powers. Rumor has it that the United States knew about the imminent attack and turned a blind eye in order to justify entering the war. But that is another story.

- The United States' new president, Harry Truman, decides to drop two atomic bombs on Japan to end the bloody war. On August 6, 1945, the Boeing B-29 known as *Enola Gay* rends the clear sky over Hiroshima. Pilot and commander Paul Tibbets pushes the red button on his stick, and the "Little Boy" bomb drops. Three days later, a second bomb, codenamed "Fat Man," detonates in Nagasaki. These two bombs are the first—and so far the only—atomic bombs used in warfare in world history. These two horrible acts turn the Japanese cities into ruins and pile the streets with at least 250,000 dead, forcing the Land of the Rising Sun to finally surrender.

- Bebop or bop, a style of jazz, surfaces in the United States in 1946. The most influential bebop artists are Charlie Parker, Dexter Gordon, Thelonious Monk, James Moody, and Dizzy Gillespie, who likes to play a trumpet that was bent in some drunken bar brawl. Unlike the dance-oriented swing, fast-tempo bebop—with its instrumental virtuosity and improvisation—seems revolutionary but lands hard on the ear of the average listener. As a result, it never becomes a commercial success. The artists who play bebop wear hats and sunglasses, and you can find them late at night in underground bars.

- In 1947, the Cold War between the Western and the Eastern

Bloc breaks out. The Soviet Union, enchanted by the universal ideas of Marxism and Leninism, opposes the United States, which embraces economic and social capitalism. It's a period of geopolitical tension between these two superpowers and their respective allies. The conflict is called the Cold War because in order to avoid the threat of nuclear destruction, the two superpowers never get into the ring to fight face-to-face.

- In 1954, Bill Haley releases the song "Rock Around the Clock," and rock and roll soon becomes a global phenomenon. This musical style combines jazz, rhythm and blues, gospel, and country and is aired for the first time on the radio by DJ Allan Freed. When the song is used as a soundtrack for the film *Blackboard Jungle*, Bill Haley becomes a swoon-worthy idol, and the roaring success sweeps the country off its feet. A bit later, this role of rock and roll icon will be played by Elvis Presley, who generates an even greater hoopla.

- The Vietnam War begins in 1955 and continues for two decades, leaving many countries on the verge of a nervous breakdown. This war is between North Vietnam, supported by USSR and China, and South Vietnam, supported by the USA and other anticommunist allies. America begins to ship soldiers to Vietnam in early 1959, and within a few years, their numbers multiply dramatically. After many soldiers die in the wild and inhospitable jungles of Indochina and Vietnam, the United States throws in the towel in April 1975.

- In the same year as the Vietnam War begins, one of the most brilliant minds of the twentieth century, Albert Einstein, passes away at seventy-six. Famous for the theory of relativity, in 1921 he was awarded the Nobel Prize in Physics for his services to theoretical physics, and especially for his discovery of the law of the photoelectric effect. Every night, he stared at the universe, excited about its immensity, but he didn't hesitate to criticize the quantum theory of the microcosm based on randomness and indeterminacy: "I, at any rate, am convinced that He [God] does not throw dice," he said. His colleague, Danish quantum physicist Niels Bohr, retorted, "Einstein, stop telling God what to do."[95]

- In October 1957, from their base in Kazakhstan, the Russians launch the first artificial satellite, Sputnik 1, into elliptical low earth orbit. Sputnik 2 follows the next month, but this time the satellite carries a stray dog named Laika. While the satellite is orbiting the planet, the dog dies. Forty years later, a monument in Moscow, Russia, honoring fallen Russian astronauts includes a statue of Laika.

- In 1958, fearing that the communists will attack from space, the United States makes a colossal investment by creating NASA (National Aeronautics and Space Administration). The independent space agency is responsible for the civil space program, aeronautics, and space research. President Eisenhower gets involved in the urgent and crucial construction and launch of the first US earth satellite, Explorer 1.

- In April 1961, Soviet cosmonaut Yuri Gagarin becomes the first human to journey into outer space and around the earth, in the Vostok 1 capsule. He is the first to see—eyes brimming with awe—the blue spherical jewel that houses humanity. He receives a number of medals and is honored and celebrated by the Soviet Union and other countries around the world. Seven years after his spaceflight, he loses his life in a plane accident due to an engine malfunction.

- In October 1962, a US spy plane spots the Russians installing ballistic missiles in the Bay of Pigs in Cuba, a response prompted by the Americans installing Jupiter missiles in their bases in England, Italy, and Turkey. The situation spins out of control. For a couple of weeks, tension builds, and across the world people

---
95 https://history.aip.org/exhibits/einstein/ae63.htm

hold their breaths. Realizing the danger of full-scale nuclear war, John F. Kennedy and Nikita Khrushchev begin to negotiate. Finally, logic wins over emotion, the skirmish ends, and the world begins to breathe again.

- In August 1963, Martin Luther King Jr. stands on the podium near the Lincoln Memorial during the March on Washington and speaks to the thrilled crowd of 200,000. The speech becomes famous all over the world for the phrase "I have a dream" and manages to influence Congress. King says, "I have a dream that my four little children will one day live in a nation where they will not be judged by the color of their skin but by their character."

- In November of the same year, during a convoy, the Irish-born thirty-fifth president of the United States, John F. Kennedy, is shot dead by a sniper and former US Marine, Lee Harvey Oswald, in Dallas, Texas. Some consider Oswald to be a Marxist, while others characterize him as a right-wing extremist. Oswald never goes to trial. During his transport to prison, surrounded by cops, journalists, and cameras, a man named Jack Ruby shoots him in the stomach and kills him. Right from the beginning, the assassination of the popular president is rumored to be the result of a government conspiracy. Though JFK's successor, Lyndon B. Johnson, launches an investigation, the incident remains unsolved to this day.

- In October 1967, Marxist, revolutionary, doctor, and guerrilla leader Ernesto Che Guevara travels to Bolivia with the intention of organizing a new revolutionary movement. While roaming the Bolivian mountains, he is wounded, captured, and killed by the Bolivian Army backed by the United States military. As proof of his death, they cut off his hands before burying his body in an unmarked grave. Thirty years later, his remains are unearthed and reburied in a ceremony in Cuba attended by Fidel Castro and thousands of Cubans. Comandante Che posthumously achieves hero status around the world and becomes a symbol of anti-imperialistic revolution.

- Amid US protests against the Vietnam War in early 1968, President Lyndon Johnson withdraws from the national election in March. Students take over Columbia University weeks later.
- When Martin Luther King is assassinated in April 1968, riots break out across the country, especially in Washington, DC, Baltimore, and Chicago. Demonstrators flow into the streets, rioting and looting. In forty-eight hours, thirty-nine civilians are killed, of which thirty-five are Black, ninety cops get wounded, and over two thousand people are arrested, including writer Normal Mailer. Soon after, he writes a book about the experience, *Armies of the Night*, which wins him a Pulitzer Prize in 1969.
- In May 1968, the worst political and social rioting since the "popular front" era of the 1930s breaks out in Paris. Today the upheaval is known as May 68. May 68 begins with a series of student protests against capitalism, consumerism, and United States imperialism. Within a few days, the rioting takes on the dimensions of a significant revolution, "punctuated by demonstrations, general strikes, and occupations of universities and factories."[96] The rapid developments force President Charles de Gaulle to declare national elections. May 68 challenges traditional institutions and defends the freedom of ideas, equality, sexuality, and human rights. Slogans include "Be realistic and demand the impossible," "Read less, live more," and "The economy is suffering, let it die."
- A year later, in 1969, American astronaut Neil Armstrong becomes the first man to walk on the moon, sealing the United States' supremacy in the Space Race. On July 20, after about four days of traveling in space, the Apollo Lunar Module lands on the moon, and as Neil Armstrong steps onto the inhospitable and

---

96 https://artsandculture.google.com/entity/may-68/m01t6ch?categoryid=event

stony ground, he famously says, "That's one small step for man, one giant leap for mankind."

- In August 1969, John Roberts, Joel Rosenman, Artie Kornfeld, and Mike Lang organize a music festival on a farm near New York City, and to their bafflement, it draws 500,000 people. The festival, called the Woodstock Music and Arts Fair, garners as much attention as the Apollo 11 moon landing. Die-hard fans storm the place to hear Carlos Santana, Janis Joplin, Jimi Hendrix, Joan Baez, Joe Cocker, the Who, and others. The Beatles, on the verge of a breakup, are nowhere in sight, while Dylan, it is said, has had enough of hippies. The place is so overcrowded that one fan says, "If you moved your leg, an arm would take its place, and that spot was gone."[97] And when a brutal thunderstorm sweeps in, all hell breaks loose. Torrential rain pummels thousands of people who have nowhere to go and turns the place into a swamp. "It sucked your shoes off," the fan continues. "It was not only mad, but it was also so dark it looked like chocolate syrup. But I've got great stories to tell, and I'm glad I was there." The ideas pervading the festival are of peace, love, and solidarity.

- In June 1970, the Beatles, the best-selling music act of all time, with 600 million records sold, break up because of artistic differences. The band came out of Liverpool in 1963 and released twelve albums within seven years. After 1966, their songs broke away from the simple pop style and walked more poetic and political paths. Bob Dylan observed them fighting for women's rights, the liberation of homosexuals, and ecology and characterized them as key representatives of youth culture. Along the way, the band won seven Grammy Awards and an Academy Award for Best Original Song Score for the 1970 documentary film *Let It Be*. Without the Beatles, the music industry would surely have turned out differently.

---

[97] https://www.history.com/news/woodstock-music-festival-conditions-1969

- In 1971, charismatic American singer and poet Jim Morrison attempts to get his life back together and move past his drinking and drug abuse by taking time off from the Doors and moving to Paris with his girlfriend, Pamela Courson. Unfortunately, months later, he dies of heart failure at the age of twenty-seven, a number that has begun to carry portentous meaning in the music world. His girlfriend finds him in the bathtub of their apartment with his eyes open. There is no autopsy. His grave is in the Père-Lachaise Cemetery, and engraved on the tombstone is the Greek phrase "Κατά τον δαίμονα εαυτού," which has generally been translated to mean "True to his own spirit." These words describe a man who always lived the way he chose, regardless of society's "musts" and labels. Club owner Sam Bernett publishes a book saying that Morrison died of a heroin overdose at his nightclub and was carried back to his apartment afterward.

    In the magnificent 1979 film *Apocalypse Now*, director Francis Ford Coppola chooses to begin the first scene of the film with the song "The End," which may be the most psychedelic moment of the whole movie and one of the best songs created by the Doors.

- In June 1972, two young, undistinguished American reporters, Carl Bernstein and Bob Woodward, team up with a secret informant nicknamed Deep Throat and uncover a major national wiretapping scandal. It all begins when five men are caught wiretapping phones and stealing documents from the Democratic National Committee's office in the Watergate office complex in Washington, DC. Though Nixon denies involvement or knowledge of the incident, the public smells a rat.

    Throughout the election campaign of the same year, Deep Throat feeds the two young reporters vital information: The burglars were not thugs. They wore expensive suits and surgical gloves and carried advanced monitoring mechanisms. Later, in the courtroom, one of the hackers claims to be a CIA security consultant. President Nixon resigns and becomes the country's first president to do so. Since then, the Watergate scandal has radically changed the way Americans view and approach politics.

- In 1972, the Dutch electronics company Philips releases the first consumer video cassette recorder. The design of the N1500 is quite sleek. The controls and its face are made of aluminum, and it is topped off with an eye-catching analogue clock. This technological breakthrough in everyday life creates a shift in television viewing. For the first time, people can record anything they fancy while they are away from home and watch it at their leisure. People can skip the commercials or run the videotape back or forward or watch it again right from the beginning or press pause and talk on the phone.

- In July of the same year, legendary American chess player Bobby Fischer wins against the Russian Boris Spassky. The notorious match takes place in the Laugardalshöll arena in Iceland, and it has been called the "Match of the Century." The twenty-nine-year-old Fisher becomes the first American to win the world title, breaking the Soviets' twenty-four-year streak. In a sense, this chess match represents a small-scale version of international political conditions.

- In March 1973, the one and only Pink Floyd, the psychedelic rock band, releases *The Dark Side of the Moon*, which becomes one of the most iconic albums in rock music. The lyrics concern the problems of everyday life, the passing of time, the greedy pursuit of money, psychedelia, and death. The songs criticize the modern and oppressive way of life, the frenzy of consumption, and military conflicts. Unique sounds are included in the music, such as the noise of a plane crash and the sound of dozens of alarm clocks going off and of coins being dropped in a cash register. *The Dark Side of the Moon,* featuring on its cover a prism that breaks a stream of light into the colors of the rainbow, becomes the most commercially successful album of all time until AC/DC's *Back in Black* is released in 1980.

- In April 1975, Bill Gates and Paul Allen found the Microsoft Corporation, a United States software company. It produces computer software, consumer electronics, personal computers, and related services. The company's best-known software products are Microsoft Office and the web browsers Internet Explorer and Edge. It remains among the five top American information technology companies, alongside Meta (Facebook), Amazon, Alphabet (Google), and Apple. Bill Gates, at the age of just thirty-one, becomes the youngest billionaire in the world.

- A year later, inventors Steve Jobs and Steve Wozniak create the first Apple computer in their garage. The name "Apple" comes from Jobs's time on the All One Farm commune in Oregon. Today, some of the company's popular products are MacBook computers, iPhones, iPads, and iPods. Steve Jobs, a Zen Buddhist, passes away in 2011 at the age of fifty-six. A visionary in the field of technology and the first person to conceive the idea of the home computer, he is christened "the great evangelist of the digital age." If you ever go to Budapest, you can see the seven-foot-tall bronze statue of Jobs created by the artist Erno Toth for Graphisoft, a Hungarian software company.

- In August 1977, Elvis Presley, born in East Tupelo, Mississippi, passes away at forty-two years old. He is found lying face down on the floor in his mansion in Memphis, Tennessee. The doctors announce that he died of heart arrhythmia owing to a large dose of drugs. His funeral becomes a national event, and millions of his fans watch it on television. He was the king of rock and roll and one of the most successful artists in the history of recorded music. As legend has it, Elvis used shoe polish on his hair.

- In July 1979, the Sony Corporation introduces the original

Walkman, a portable cassette player that allows people to listen to music on the move. This handheld device astonishes people to the same degree that cellular phones and digital cameras will later. We owe the invention of this amazing gadget to legendary chairman Masaru Ibuka, a music lover and avid traveler who tasked deputy Norio Ohga with putting together a device that could be easily carried around. Just four months later, Sony engineers have a reliable product that costs 30,000 yen, or 150 dollars. Walkman hits the market before the start of summer vacation for Japanese students.

- In the same year, Pink Floyd releases one of the most intriguing and imaginative albums in the history of rock music, *The Wall*. The album has elements reminiscent of a theatrical performance and talks about abandonment, isolation, and neo-Nazism. The idea for the album hit Roger Waters during a concert. He imagined a wall between himself and the audience that had disappointed him. *The Wall* also speaks of loved ones killed during the Second World War, the obsolete educational system, and the overprotective mother figure. In 1982, the great director Alan Parker brings *The Wall* to the screen, and Waters later releases two DVDs immortalizing his fantastic musical theater show: *Live in Berlin* (1990), and *The Wall* (2014).

- In snowy December 1980, tragedy shakes the world. John Lennon, a founding member of the Beatles and an activist with a strong social sensitivity who was considered one of the leading figures in the protests against the Vietnam War, is shot dead by a disturbed fan. Only a decade after the breakup of the Beatles, Lennon has made a name for himself as a successful solo artist. According to eyewitnesses, after committing the terrible act, twenty-five-year-old Mark Chapman squats on the sidewalk and reads J. D. Salinger's *Catcher in the Rye* until the police surge in, sirens howling.

Singer and songwriter James Taylor shares that he met David Chapman a day before the murder. He says, "His assassin had buttonholed me in the tube station. He pinned me to the wall, glistening with maniacal sweat, and tried to talk in some freak speech about what he was gonna do, and stuff about how John was interested and how he was gonna get in touch with John Lennon. It was surreal to have contact with the guy twenty-four hours before he shot John."[98] Two months prior to the murder, Chapman told his wife, Gloria Hiroko, that he was planning to kill the artist to make a name for himself.

- In August 1981, the channel MTV (Music Television) is launched in New York City. "Ladies and gentlemen, rock and roll" are the first words spoken on MTV, by John Lack. By broadcasting popular music and music videos twenty-four seven, the channel changes the way the average person perceives the music industry. The music videos are aired by personalities known as video jockeys, or VJs. The first video is for the Buggles' "Video Killed the Radio Star," which has symbolic importance. MTV brings about a revolution. For the first time, music fans can view the music of their choice from the comfort of their homes.

- Whether you know her as Madame X, the Material Girl, or the star of *Shanghai Surprise*, you certainly know Madonna, who comes into the spotlight in the early 1980s. A prolific American singer, songwriter, dancer, and actress with Italian roots, she becomes famous by constantly renewing her image and for her groundbreaking videos and unique voice. She is the queen of pop and one of the biggest cultural symbols on the planet. In 2008, Madonna is inducted into the Rock & Roll Hall of Fame. As of today, she has sold 340 million albums and holds the record as the highest-grossing solo touring artist of all time.

---

98   https://www.realclearhistory.com/2020/12/08/lennons_killer_chickened_out_before_first_attempt_652236.html

- In July 1985, to raise money for the famine sweeping through Ethiopia, two historic concerts known as Live Aid are organized, one at Wembley Stadium in London and the other at John F. Kennedy Stadium in Philadelphia. It is a global sensation as seventy-five top acts perform and are watched on television by two billion fans worldwide.

    As expected, Queen's Freddie Mercury steals the show. Ronnie Wood performs an epic air guitar because he hands his real guitar to Bob Dylan, who broke a string. Elton John wears a chef's hat and barbecues backstage while Phil Collins, who plays at both gigs, says, "I was in England this afternoon. Funny old world, innit?"[99] A young Madonna is described as an up-and-coming star, and when Freddie Mercury sees David Bowie decked out in a blue suit, he says, "If I didn't know you better, I'd have to eat you." And the Pretenders rehearse in a nearby pub because all the places are fully booked. The total amount of money raised by these two incredible concerts is 127 million dollars.

- In 1986, seeking to bring the Soviet Union up to date with countries like Germany, Japan, China, and the United States, President Mikhail Gorbachev announces perestroika, which means reconstruction with regard to the economic, political, and social system of the country. Disapproving of Marxist and Leninist theories, Gorbachev redistributes land for private use, reorganizes economic controls, and urges enterprises to become self-financing. While the economic bureaucracy of the country tries to block most of his reforms, he suggests reducing the direct involvement of the Communist Party leadership in the country's governance and increasing the local government's authority instead. Though a new parliament, the Soviet Congress of People's Deputies, is successfully created in 1988, giving the people the choice to vote for different noncommunist candidates, the Communist Party

---

99   https://m.imdb.com/title/tt0261024/quotes/?item=qt0199771

continues to hold the reins tight.

- In April 1986, the world's worst nuclear disaster happens in Chernobyl, an area of the Soviet Union now belonging to Ukraine. A reactor blows up, spewing a cloud of radioactive material into the atmosphere that spreads across Northern and Western Europe and all the way to the United States. The level of radiation is similar to that of Hiroshima. In the following years, the United Nations Committee on the Effects of Atomic Radiation reports that six thousand children and adults have developed different forms of cancer.

  The evacuated area surrounding Chernobyl becomes known as the Red Forest because many of the trees turn reddish brown and wither away. Though some species thrive, the radiation causes significant and deadly abnormalities; for example, birds suffer from deformed beaks, elevated levels of cataracts, albinism, and lower rates of beneficial bacteria. In 2011, Ukraine opens the exclusion area to tourism. Despite it being illegal, about 150 people still live in the area. Most residents are women who still farm their land.

- Also in 1986, the British Pet Shop Boys, who a place in the Guinness Book of Records as the most commercially successful duo in their country, resurrect disco music.

  First emerging in the 1970s, disco is a beat-driven style of music that combines elements of funk, soul, and Latin music. Mostly enjoyed by the underground subculture, disco became a significant musical movement, encouraging people to dance as a group and not just as a couple. You could say that disco was a reaction against the conservatism and rock music that previously dominated the music scene.

  In its heyday, disco promoted a new kind of nightlife, full of challenges and unrestrained pleasures. Under the swirling, multicolored lights and revolving disco balls of Studio 54, which opened in 1924 in New York and was shut down in 1980, people danced the night away, enjoying plenty of alcohol, drugs, and sex. By turning the records on turntables, disc jockeys elevated Donna Summer, Gloria Gaynor, and the Bee Gees to stardom.

- In 1989, the World Wide Web breaks into the market. This open system of interconnected information allows people to search for information, send data, and communicate across a network. British computer scientist Tim Berners-Lee creates it while working at CERN (European Center for Nuclear Research) in Geneva, Switzerland. In 2016, he is awarded the Turing Prize (named for the mathematician Alan Turing, father of computer science and artificial intelligence). This annual American award grants high academic distinction, like a Nobel Prize in computer science, and comes with a million-dollar award.

    Over the years, Berners-Lee watches his creation evolve into a force he could never have imagined. On the day of the World Wide Web's thirtieth birthday, he writes, "While the web has created opportunity, given marginalized groups a voice, and made our daily lives easier, it has also created an opportunity for scammers, given a voice to those who spread hatred, and made all kinds of crime easier to commit."[100]

- In November 1989, the Berlin Wall, the fifteen-foot-tall and ninety-six-mile-long monster that has separated friends and families over three decades, finally falls. More than five thousand people managed to escape over or under the iconic barbed-wired Cold War symbol, and more than one hundred died. East Germans call the Wall the antifascist bulwark, and the Western Germans call it the "Wall of Shame." Built in August 1961 in the center of Berlin by the East Germans, it was intended to limit the increasing number of citizens moving to the West.

---

100   https://webfoundation.org/2019/03/web-birthday-30/

The Wall symbolizes the political and ideological division of the Cold War. Two years after the Wall's destruction, the German band Scorpions writes the ballad "Wind of Change."

- In August 1990, Iraq, under the leadership of Saddam Hussein, invades Kuwait under the pretext that their neighbors are stealing oil from the Al-Rumaylah oil field, which lies on the border between the two countries. The Persian War, or Gulf War, breaks out. Fearing that Saddam will try to invade Saudi Arabia—thereby gaining control of more than 40 percent of the world's oil reserves, as well as two of the holiest cities in the Islamic world, Mecca and Edina—the United States, backed by thirty-five countries, rapidly deploys its mighty war machine to the Persian Gulf. Operation Desert Storm (air bombardment) and Operation Desert Sabre (ground assault) involve the largest military coalition since WWII, and it is the first war to be televised live by CNN. Though Kuwait is liberated, Saddam's regime remains in power in Iraq.

- In September 1991, Guns N' Roses releases a double album, *Use Your Illusion*. The band formed in 1985 in LA in a small apartment called "Hell House," where there were plenty of drugs, girls, and alcohol. In the grooves of the records, two wonderful arrangements are carved: "Live and Let Die" by Paul McCartney, which played in the 1973 James Bond film, and Bob Dylan's "Knockin' on Heaven's Door," a song that writer Clinton Heylin describes as an exercise in splendid simplicity.[101] Guns N' Roses is one of the best hard rock bands in the world, and it is important to note that these two music giants introduce them to a younger audience. "November Rain"—a nine-minute song composed by Axl Rose over a ten-year stretch—becomes a huge hit. As of today, Guns N' Roses has released six albums and is considered one of the world's top-selling bands of all time.

---

101 https://americansongwriter.com/behind-the-history-and-meaning-of-the-song-knockin-on-heavens-door-by-bob-dylan/

- Two months later, Freddie Mercury, a charismatic artist with an exceptional and versatile voice and one of the most colorful performers of all time, dies of AIDS. Though he spoke in a baritone range, he sang in the tenor range. Freddie became famous through the British rock band Queen, which he formed in 1970. Queen's greatest song, "Bohemian Rhapsody," from the 1975 album *A Night at the Opera*, has over the years been subject to myriad interpretations. It is six minutes long and combines polyphonic choir, ballad, musical, opera, and hard rock. Though Elton John thinks that the song is ridiculous, "Bohemian Rhapsody" has become one of the most popular songs of the twentieth century.[102]

- In December 1991, the Soviet Union dissolves, effectively ending the forty-year-long Cold War with the United States. In the years to come, Soviet satellite states Armenia, Azerbaijan, Belarus, Lithuania, Moldova, Russia, Tajikistan, Turkmenistan, Ukraine, and Uzbekistan become independent. Before Gorbachev, the eighth and last leader of the Soviet Union, resigns and hands power over to Boris Yeltsin, he gives a final speech and tries to explain what went wrong. His words are laced with regret and frustration. Gorbachev admits that communism has failed and that Russia shall become a democratic country. On this chilly night in December, with the streets and parks in Moscow covered in snow, the Kremlin takes down the Soviet flag and raises the Russian one, thus burying the Cold War.

- In 1993, Nelson Mandela and Frederik de Klerk win the Nobel Peace Prize. The former is a campaigner and the first non-White president of South Africa, and the latter is the country's last president during the apartheid regime. Apartheid, which means segregation, was at its height a White man's authoritarian political structure that enforced racial discrimination. Led by the Dutch in South Africa from 1948 to 1994, this racial hierarchy placed

---

102 https://www.radiox.co.uk/artists/queen/elton-john-bohemian-rhapsody-absolutely-ridiculous/

White people at the top and Black people at rock bottom, where they lacked basic needs like proper housing and education and freedom of speech and movement. Relationships between Whites and Blacks were strictly forbidden. If a child was born out of such a union, the family was separated, and the Black individual was thrown in jail. Many violent protests, strikes, and demonstrations were dealt with through severe governmental brutality. The most violent protest took place on March 21, 1960, when police officers opened fire and killed sixty-nine Africans. It is important to mention that not all Whites living in South Africa during that time supported apartheid.

- A year later, in 1994, the lead singer and guitarist of the famous American band Nirvana, Kurt Cobain, is found dead in his home in Seattle with a gun in his hand. He is only twenty-seven years old. In Buddhism, Nirvana is a transcendent state where there is neither suffering nor desire nor any sense of self. A person becomes one with the universe and experiences total bliss.

  Kurt formed Nirvana in 1987, and it became one of the most successful grunge bands, creating a bridge between mainstream 1980s heavy metal/hard rock and postpunk alternative rock. Grunge flourished in Seattle, where Microsoft's growth became a magnet for record executives looking for the next big thing. In the following years, grunge became an international fad. Right from the start, Kurt was considered a spokesman of Generation X. He had a great ability to influence the youth, and "Smells Like Teen Spirit," from the album *Nevermind*, elevated his reputation to that of a guru. The editor of *Rolling Stone* magazine called Kurt Cobain the John Lennon of grunge. When Bob Dylan heard Kurt singing "Polly," a song that tells a true and tough story, he said, "The kid has heart."

  After his death, grunge slowly but steadily fades away. Before we move on, I believe that it is worth our time to read excerpts from Kurt Cobain's suicide note: [103]

> I haven't felt the excitement of listening to as well as creating music along with reading and writing for too many years now. I feel guilty beyond words about these things. When we're backstage and the lights go out and the manic roar of the crowds begins, it doesn't affect me the way in which it did for Freddie Mercury, who seemed to love, and relish in the love and adoration from the crowd which is something I totally admire and envy.
>
> I can't fool you, any one of you. It simply isn't fair to you or me. The worst crime I can think of would be to rip people off by faking it and pretending as if I'm having 100% fun.
>
> I've had a much better appreciation for all the people I've known personally, and as fans of our music, but I still can't get over the frustration, guilt, and empathy I have for everyone. There's good in all of us and I think I simply love people too much, so much that it makes me feel too fucking sad. The sad little, sensitive, unappreciative, Pisces, Jesus man. Why don't you just enjoy it? I don't know!
>
> Thank you all from the pit of my burning, nauseous stomach for your letters and concern during the past years. I'm too much of an erratic, moody baby! I don't have the passion anymore, so remember, it's better to burn out than to fade away.
>
> Peace, love, empathy.
> Kurt Cobain

- In 1996, in foggy Edinburg, Scotland, Dolly the sheep, the first cloned mammal, is born. Dolly is named after famous country

---

103 https://tribune.com.pk/story/2293323/on-this-day-grunge-icon-kurt-cobain-pulls-the-trigger

singer Dolly Parton. This scientific breakthrough instantly catches the spotlight. Six years later, and after giving birth to six lambs, Dolly develops lung cancer and arthritis. Her cells also age extremely quickly compared to those of normal sheep. She is euthanized, and so the bold experiment ends.

- In May 1997, world chess champion Garry Kasparov battles the US Deep Blue computer produced by IBM. This is a monumental moment in chess history. The eyes of the world are fixed on the iconic series of games. Kasparov wins the one in Philadelphia, and in the second game, played in New York City, Deep Blue wins. The computer's first historic win has symbolic significance in its suggestion that artificial intelligence may be catching up to human intelligence.

  After his defeat, Kasparov angrily claims that during critical moments of the game where intuition played an important part, the computer movements were secretly controlled by humans, whom Kasparov believes hid in another room. When the world chess champion asks for a rematch, IBM refuses and disassembles the machine.

- In 2001, American singer, songwriter, and guitarist John Phillips passes away at the age of sixty-five. The leader of the Mamas & the Papas composed the hippie anthem "San Francisco (Be Sure to Wear Flowers in Your Hair)," which was performed for the first time by Scott McKenzie in 1967.

- In September 2001, nineteen militants linked with the Islamic extremist group al-Qaeda hijack four civilian planes, crashing two of them into the Twin Towers (World Trade Center), one into Pentagon headquarters, and the last one, after an attempt by the passengers to take control, into a field near Pennsylvania. It is the deadliest terrorist attack on American soil and in the country's history. Some 2,750 people are killed in New York City, 184 at the Pentagon, and 40 outside Pennsylvania. More than 400 police officers and firefighters are also killed in the aftermath.

- In February 2004, Mark Zuckerberg, a student at Harvard University, with the help of fellow students, creates Facebook, an online social media and networking service. It is named after the directories provided by the universities to their students. Over the years, Facebook has been criticized for causing addiction and low self-esteem and for posting fake news, hate speeches, and conspiracy theories. Facebook is where you can go to spy on your ex, send messages, chat with your friends, post selfies, and other curiosities. If you're a seller, it's a platform with 2.8 billion potential customers.

- In December of the same year, a powerful undersea earthquake with a magnitude of 9.1 shakes the islands of Sumatra and Simeulue of Indonesia. Over the next seven hours, a tsunami triggered by the earthquake sends thirty-foot waves toward coastal areas as far away as East Africa, causing unparalleled destruction and chaos. It is the worst natural disaster of the twentieth century. The raging tsunami kills at least 225,000 people in Indonesia, Shri Lanka, India, Maldives, and Thailand. It is the first time a tsunami has been videotaped. It's worth mentioning that shortly before the disaster, several animals, especially the elephants of the area, fled the coasts, heading for the slopes or nearby forests.

- In August 2005, Hurricane Katrina, one of the strongest hurricane cyclones in history, strikes the southeastern United States, causing tremendous disaster and deaths. The storm surfaces near the Bahamas, 350 miles east of Miami, and over the next two days grows in strength. Ninety-five-mile winds lash Florida. A couple of days later, with winds reaching 175 miles per hour, Katrina sweeps through Louisiana and crushes New Orleans, leaving hundreds of thousands of people homeless and almost two thousand dead.

- In 2008, global investment bank Lehman Brothers, established in 1844 by a German family, drops to its knees. Hundreds of employees decked out in suits leave the bank carrying cardboard boxes. Lehman Brothers is a giant on the same scale as the investment bank Goldman Sachs. The bankruptcy of Lehman Brothers represents the beginning of the global financial crisis that in the following years will almost wipe out the middle class and stretch the gap between rich and poor even further.

- In August 2009, Barack Obama becomes the forty-fourth president of the United States and the first African American politician to achieve such a remarkable victory. Obama is a member of the Democratic Party and was a member of the Illinois Senate. In October 2009, he wins the Nobel Peace Prize for working to end nuclear proliferation.

    Obama also cuts unemployment from 10 percent to 4.9 percent, and the deficit from 9.8 percent to just 2.5 percent. Clean energy begins to power American homes and businesses. In 2010, Obama signs and implements the Affordable Care Act to cut health care costs. He declares that health care is not a privilege for a few but a right for all. With the help of his wife, he signs the Healthy, Hunger-Free Kids Act and injects 4.5 billion dollars into school lunch programs. More troops come home to their families after the Iraq War ends in 2011 following the death of Osama bin Laden, and Obama increases benefits for US veterans. He passes drastic banking reforms to prevent abusive loan practices and misuse of bank capital. And finally, he improves the United States' image abroad.

- In June 2009, the controversial "King of Pop," Michael Jackson, passes away at fifty-one. A charismatic composer, singer, dancer, and actor, he managed to exploit his musical expertise like no one had before. "Billy Jean" was the first song by a Black artist to be aired on MTV. His album *Thriller* was a worldwide hit, selling about sixty-five million copies. MJ has twenty-three Guinness

Records, forty Billboard Awards, thirteen Grammys, and twenty-six American Music Awards. During his life, he underwent several face operations to get white skin and finer features. His record sales exceed 750 million copies to date. "Heal the World," "They Don't Care About Us," and "Earth Song" carry social messages. MJ is considered to be the most significant cultural icon of the twentieth century.

- In December 2011, scientists at CERN (European Center for Nuclear Research) discover the Higgs boson or God particle, which was first theorized in a scientific paper written by Peter Higgs in 1964. It is a great scientific achievement in the quantum world because being able to measure the properties of the Higgs boson in detail will help scientists further explore many mysteries in particle physics and cosmology. For instance, what existed before the big bang?

- In 2012, *Voyager 1*, a robotic interplanetary probe, exits our solar system and enters interstellar space. Launched in September 1977 from Cape Canaveral in the United States, its mission has been to travel into unknown and uncharted space, collect data, and send it back to Earth. In its belly, *Voyager 1* carries pictures of Earth's mountains, plains, and seas, along with a twelve-inch gold-plated record containing greetings in fifty different languages; nature sounds like wind and thunder; and animal sounds, such as a lion's roar. It also carries nine minutes of music by Johann Sebastian Bach, Igor Stravinsky, Chuck Berry, Aboriginal Indigenous Australians, etc.

- In April 2013 in London, Margaret Thatcher passes away from a stroke at the age of eighty-eight. Known as the "Iron Lady," she was the first female prime minister of England and presided from 1979 to 1990. She had strong political views and believed in deregulation and the privatization of state-owned companies. Trying to revive the wounded English economy, she limited the role of the state in the world of business and implemented neoliberal ideas inspired by the economist Milton Friedman of the Chicago School. It is worth mentioning that Friedman's economic theories had been most recently put into practice by Chile's dictator, Auguste Pinochet, who happened to be Thatcher's friend.

- In November 2016, beloved Canadian poet, novelist, singer, and songwriter Leonard Cohen dies at eighty-two in Los Angeles. His songs or ballads carry an existential bite, with roots in European cabaret, something which established him as one of the most distinctive voices of 1970s pop music. The lyrics of his songs talk about religion, love, loneliness, sexuality, loss, depression, death, and romantic relationships. Cohen was a strong opponent of war and abortion. His song "Dance Me to the End of Love" is believed to be an anthem against the death and horror of Nazi crematoria. In 2010 he won a Grammy for his work. He is in the Canadian Songwriters Hall of Fame and the Rock & Roll Hall of Fame. He had a house in Hydra, Greece, where he loved to spend time.

- In 2017, American guitarist and rock and roll composer Chuck Berry dies at ninety-one. Through his songs "Roll Over Beethoven" and "Johnny B. Goode," he became famous among the younger generations. John Lennon once said, "If you tried to give rock and roll another name, you might call it 'Chuck Berry.'"[104] His work was influenced by the blues, which in turn influenced the British bands the Rolling Stones and the Animals. *Rolling Stone* magazine names him among the greatest guitarists of all time. In 1986, he was inducted into the Rock & Roll Hall of Fame. Former president Clinton said after Berry's death: "Hillary and I loved Chuck Berry for as long as we can remember. The man was inseparable from his music—both were utterly original and distinctly American. He made our feet move and our hearts more joyful. And along the way, he changed our country and the history

---

104   https://edition.cnn.com/2017/03/18/entertainment/chuck-berry-reactions-social-media-trnd/index.html

of popular music."[105]

- In March of the same year, English theoretical physicist Stephen Hawking passes away at seventy-six. He is known for his progressive theories on black holes, drawing upon relativity theory and quantum mechanics. In the early 1960s, Hawking was diagnosed with amyotrophic lateral sclerosis, a disease that over the years paralyzed his entire body and put him in a wheelchair. His book *A Brief History of Time: From the Big Bang to Black Holes* (1988) became a bestseller with over twenty-five million copies sold. The book talks about the structure, origin, development, and eventual fate of the universe, about space and time, quarks and gravity, and about the big bang and black holes. Hawkins also discusses general relativity and quantum mechanics. And finally, he talks about his unifying theory of the universe. He wrote the book for readers who have no prior knowledge of physics.

  Responding to Einstein and Bohr's beliefs about whether God played dice while creating the universe, Hawking had this to say: "Not only does God play dice, but he sometimes throws them where they cannot be seen."[106]

---

105   https://www.billboard.com/music/rock/the-clintons-pay-tribute-to-chuck-berry-7728721/
106   https://www.brainyquote.com/quotes/stephen_hawking_131084

MORE BACK PAGES

"I accept chaos. I'm not sure whether it accepts me."[107]

Bob Dylan

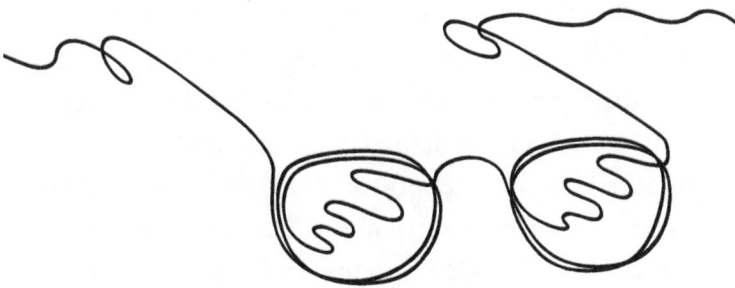

---
107 https://www.goodreads.com/quotes/21438-i-accept-chaos-i-m-not-sure-whether-it-accepts-me

SYMBOLISM IN LITERATURE

BOB DYLAN IS not just a great musician whose only concern is the musical heritage of his country. Throughout his prolific career, Dylan has explored many lyrical themes and written many masterpieces where you can find poetic and literary traces inspired by Arthur Rimbaud and Charles Baudelaire. Many of his songs, including "Maggie's Farm," "Ballad of a Thin Man," "Desolation Row," "Visions of Johana," "Homesick Blues," and "Farewell, Angelina," involve symbolic and surrealistic elements. The artists of his youth inspired him as much as Dylan inspired others. His literary fingerprint is everywhere. No other living artist has managed to dig so deep into the American heart and soul.

Now we are going to take a little dive into symbolism and surrealism and read a few more songs written by Bob Dylan.

~

Symbolism is a literary device that can enhance and elevate a deeper or hidden message. It all began with the French artists. The leading symbolists were Charles Baudelaire, Arthur Rimbaud, Paul Verlaine, Stéphane Mallarmé, and Paul Valery, eminent and distinguished poets of the nineteenth century. They used symbols borrowed from the material and spiritual worlds to convey their thoughts, moods, and emotions. In doing so, they highlighted deeper meanings. For instance, sunrise can symbolize birth and life, and sunset death. Rain is often a symbol of sadness.

Symbolism was born as a reaction against naturalism and realism. It is similar to metaphor and allegory, but allegories contain elements of didacticism and so fail to capture what is transcendent about reality in the mysterious and magical ways symbolism does.

Like metaphors, symbols work best when they appear at key points in poems, short stories, novellas, and novels. Excessive use of symbolism should be avoided because touching base with reality in the text is necessary in order for symbols to carry across their intended meaning.

Symbolic thinking appeared before the genesis of language, emerging in caves where *Homo sapiens* used colors to paint, with each color having its own meaning, usually to do with prevailing hierarchical relationships. Symbolism in religion frequently involves sacrifice, death, and resurrection. Often, to achieve a higher humanistic purpose, someone or something must be sacrificed to purify one's body, mind, and spirit.

Another font of symbols is numbers. Repetition of numbers can lace the work with mystique and magic. For example, the number seven is often associated with the seven deadly sins (pride, greed, envy, wrath, laziness, gluttony, and lust), and four might represent the four main dimensions of our physical world (length, width, height, time, according to Einstein), the four cardinal directions (east, west, north, south), and the basic elements of nature (earth, water, fire, air). The number three can symbolize birth, life, and death; mind, soul, and body; past, present, and future. Pythagoras talks about the beginning, middle, and end and also about the states of matter (solid, liquid, gas).

Related to numbers is the concept of time. The sun and moon, for example, both serve to measure time, suggesting that numbers not only define space and time but are also part of one enigmatic universe, connecting our lives with planets, stars, solar systems, and galaxies.

Colors also have great power in the world of symbolism. They influence our moods, emotions, and behavior. Some common associations are as follows: red stands for fire, passion, fury, heat; pink represents femininity and youthfulness; orange symbolizes warmth, activity, and vitality; yellow usually symbolizes cheerfulness, friendliness, joy, good luck, and richness; blue symbolizes royalty, business, reliability, and trustworthiness, but it can also symbolize sadness and depression; purple stands for majesty, nobility, luxury, and mystery; brown symbolizes orderliness, strength, and honesty; and green symbolizes rebirth, vitality, prestige, and wealth.

An understanding of symbolism helps readers and listeners contemplate an artist's work in depth.

ARTHUR RIMBAUD

(1854–1891)

"One night I sat Beauty on my knees—And I found her bitter—And I reviled her."[108]

THE GREAT WRITER Victor Hugo once compared Jean Nicolas Arthur Rimbaud to an infant Shakespeare because he wrote many influential poems before turning twenty. Rimbaud was born in Charleville, France, and is considered one of the top representatives of symbolism. His best work, and the only one he published by choice, was *A Season in Hell*.

When he turned seven, his father abandoned the family. The poet's Catholic mother, a strong-willed woman, undertook the upbringing, education, and training of her five children. Under the constant guidance of his mother, whom in one of his letters he called "imperial prosecutor," the outwardly pious and obedient Rimbaud astonished his teachers at the College de Charleville with his brilliance in many subjects, especially literature. He was a voracious reader, and winning first prize for a Latin poem in 1870 gave Rimbaud confidence and the burning ambition to become acknowledged by the Parnassian poets.

By the time he turned sixteen, he had developed a distinctive voice. In his poems, you discover a rebelliousness toward his hometown environment and a desire for adventure, freedom, and transcendence. He hated hypocrisy, apathy, self-satisfaction, and sentimental clichés.

At the College de Charleville, Rimbaud met Professor Georges

---

[108] https://www.goodreads.com/quotes/414487-one-evening-i-sat-beauty-on-my-knees-and

Izambard, who recognized the young poet's talent and helped him greatly by providing him with books and giving him tips on how to improve his writing. At sixteen, Rimbaud left his maternal home and secretly traveled by train to Paris to meet his beloved professor. Since he didn't pay the fare, officers threw him in jail, but after two days, they sent him to Izambard, who paid for his release. Arthur spent some time working by the professor's side.

Back home, his mother pressured him to get a job. Instead, Rimbaud wrote an autobiographical letter to the poet Paul Verlaine and sent it to him, including some of his poems. Verlaine was excited by Rimbaud's talent and vision and paid for the would-be poet's ticket to Paris, then put him up in his own home where he lived with his wife and child.

Keeping in touch with the Parnassians,[109] Rimbaud tried to worm his way into the literary elite but didn't succeed. His attitude, private life, and provocative and brash character generated strong reactions and negative impressions among the elite. Combined with his homosexuality and anarchism, these qualities pushed the young Arthur to the margins of society. A period of volatile passion occurred between Rimbaud and Verlaine, with Verlaine torn between his sexual partner and his family. Their short affair ended disastrously after the two men traveled to Brussels. One night, after a fight in a bistro, Verlaine shot Rimbaud in his arm and spent two years in prison. Rimbaud returned home and, during his recovery, finished the famous *A Season in Hell*. After traveling to different countries, Rimbaud joined the Dutch Colonial Army, then deserted, and later worked as an interpreter and an arms dealer.

In his letter known as "I Is Another," Rimbaud makes it his supreme duty to discover himself. In a series of letters known as "Letters of the Seer," he presents his artistic vision, saying that he feels

---

109 Parnassism was a literary movement that developed in France in the nineteenth century. Its name is borrowed from the Greek mountain Parnassos, where, according to mythology, the muses lived. Parnassism reacted to the emotional excess of romance and took refuge in the other extreme, apathy.

more like a prophet who seeks the unknown and a new way of looking at the world than a poet. Through his writing, he explored his vision in a way that transcended reality, leading him to incredible spiritual, psychological, and emotional highs.

After wandering Africa without taking care of his health, Rimbaud became ill. The doctors told him he was suffering from cancer in his bones, and they were forced to amputate his right leg. In a few months, lying in bed half-paralyzed, the poet died. His body was taken to Charleville, and on the tombstone was engraved PRAY FOR HIM.

An amalgam of Apollo and Dionysus, Don Quixote and Odysseus, Arthur Rimbaud wanted to be a prophet. He strongly believed in a universal life force, which could be sensed only by the chosen few. Through his own consciousness, he wanted to infuse his poems with the music of the universe so his fellow men could experience spiritual awakening, which in turn would drive them toward social progress. Rimbaud was a modernist, breaking through the barriers of traditional metric forms and, with the help of his strange visions and constant search for the unknown, filling his work with fantastic new shapes and forms. His work influenced the surrealists André Breton, Tristan Tzara, and Paul Èluard and the writers of the Beat generation, as well as famous musicians such as Jim Morrison, John Lennon, and Bob Dylan.

"Maggie's Farm" (Lyrics)[110]

> I ain't gonna work on Maggie's farm no more
> No, I ain't gonna work on Maggie's farm no more
> Well, I wake up in the morning, fold my hands and pray for rain
> I got a head full of ideas that are drivin' me insane
> It's a shame, the way she makes me scrub the floor

---

110   Dylan, Bob, Maggie's Farm, on *Bringing It All Back Home*, Columbia, 1965. (The song is probably inspired by the book *Animal Farm* by George Orwell published in 1945, a novel that satirizes labor exploitation and Stalinist bureaucracy. It remained on the list of banned books throughout the Eastern Bloc until 1989)

I ain't gonna work on Maggie's farm no more

I ain't gonna work for Maggie's brother no more
No, I ain't gonna work for Maggie's brother no more
Well, he hands you a nickel, he hands you a dime
He asks you with a grin if you're havin' a good time
Then he fines you every time you slam the door
I ain't gonna work for Maggie's brother no more

I ain't gonna work for Maggie's pa no more
No, I ain't gonna work for Maggie's pa no more
Well, he puts his cigar out in your face, just for kicks
His bedroom window, it is made out of bricks
The National Guard stands around his door
I ain't gonna work for Maggie's pa no more

I ain't gonna work for Maggie's ma no more
No, I ain't gonna work for Maggie's ma no more
Well, she talks to all the servants about man and God and law
Everybody says she's the brains behind pa
She's sixty-eight, but she says she's fifty-four
I ain't gonna work for Maggie's ma no more

I ain't gonna work on Maggie's farm no more
I ain't gonna work on Maggie's farm no more
Well, I try my best to be just like I am
But everybody wants you to be just like them
They say, "Sing while you slave" and I just get bored
I ain't gonna work on Maggie's farm no more

SURREALISM IN LITERATURE

SURREALISM ENTERED LITERATURE in France at the beginning of the twentieth century and gained popularity during World War I. It takes its name after the French word "*sur*," which means "above," and "*réalisme*," which means "realism." We can explain the specific concept as something that exists beyond reality—something bizarre, strange, and absurd. Applying the technique of surrealism, the artist promotes personal psychic investigation and revelation.

The French poet Guillaume Apollinaire invented and used the word "surreal" to describe his theater drama *The Breasts of Tiresias* in 1917. With the intention of changing traditions, establishing equality between the sexes, and gaining power among men, Thérèse changes her sex. Apollinaire reversed the myth to create a provocative interpretation using pacifist and feminist elements. However, the famous poet André Breton was the mind behind surrealism as a full-fledged movement capable of standing on its own feet.

According to Breton,[111] surrealism is a psychic automatism trying to express itself through art and letters, setting aside logic as well as all social and moral barriers so that the endless source of the unconscious mind can begin to release thoughts, ideas, and images from a higher reality and from the world of fantasy and dreams.

The core of surrealism centers on Freud's theories about the use of dreams—not for therapeutic purposes but with the intention to release human imagination. The goal of this revolutionary movement was to melt away the barriers of reason, bring about changes in thought and art, and to provide solutions to the basic problems of

---

111   http://www.inmaterial.com/jjimenez/sysen.htm

life, such as in the aftermath of World War I amid the degeneration of universal principles and values.

Influenced by symbolism, German Romanticism, and the English gothic novel—and Rimbaud's "Let us change life" slogan and Marx's "Let us change the world"—the French surrealists used anarchism as a leftist weapon and the magazine *Litterature* to react against the destruction of rigid rationalism and social and political conventions between 1919 and 1924. In the beginning, *Litterature* was under the control of Louis Aragon, Philippe Soupault, and André Breton. But once Tristan Tzara, the founder of Dadaism, joined the movement, the writings became more revolutionary and critical of the establishment—notably the idleness of the bourgeoisie and their stiff rationalism.

After the global financial crash in 1929, the surrealists officially joined the Communist Party in France and published the magazine *Surrealism in Service of the Revolution*. The leftist bureaucracy was cautious about going after them because several of these artists belonged to the bourgeoisie.

André Breton and Philippe Soupault developed and applied the method of automatic writing in their work *Les Champs Magnétiques* ("The Magnetic Fields") in 1920. It became famous as the first work of literary surrealism that captured the unconscious, annihilated logic, and embraced nonconformism. Here is an excerpt:[112]

> It was the end of sorrowful lies. The rail stations were dead, flowing like bees stung from honeysuckle. The people hung back and watched the ocean, animals flew in and out of focus. The time had come. Yet king dogs never grow old—they stay young and fit, and someday they might come to the beach and have a few drinks, a few laughs, and get on with it. But not now. The time had come; we all knew it. But who would go first?

---

112   https://en.wikipedia.org/wiki/Les_Champs_magn%C3%A9tiques

A similar book, *Blast Furnace*, was published in Greece in 1935 by the surrealist Andreas Embiricos. No poet before, and no one ever since, had written a book so sacrilegious, so cryptic, and so incomprehensible. The book quickly sold 200 copies because it was considered a scandalous book written by a "madman," as the poet himself recalled.

In March 1922, Breton became the director of *Litterature*, and a month later, a definitive rupture with Dadaism occurred, which Breton publicly announced. One of the reasons Breton broke off his relations with Dadaism was because of its nihilism. In the next two years and through international conferences in which artists of cubism and futurism participated, surrealism took its final form. Breton, Éluard, Aragon, and Max Ernst, to name a few, began experimenting with automatism, dreams, hypnotism, and drugs, but when mass suicide attempts by hypnotized followers occurred, the experiment came to a halt. In the first *Manifesto of Surrealism*, Breton rejects the mechanical aid of drugs and of hypnotism. In addition, Breton expresses a strong dissatisfaction toward Christianity and Cartesianism, for they likewise confuse and weaken the human mind and spirit.

Some great painters and sculptors who embraced surrealism include René Magritte, Marcel Duchamp, Joan Miró, Henry Moore, Alberto Giacometti, and Nikos Engonopoulos.

Quite a few art historians have noted that after the rise of Nazism in 1933 and especially during World War II, surrealism began to decline. And three years after André Breton passed away in 1969, surrealism as an organized literary movement officially came to an end.

"Ballad of a Thin Man" (Lyrics)[113]

You walk into the room
With your pencil in your hand
You see somebody naked and you
You say, "Who is that man?"
You try so hard, but you don't understand
Just what you will say when you get home
Because something is happening here
But you don't know what it is
Do you, Mister Jones?

You raise up your head
And you ask, "Is this where it is?"
And somebody points to you and says, "It's his"
And you say, "What's mine?"
And somebody else says, "Where what is?"
And you say, "Oh, my God, am I here all alone?"
But something is happening
And you don't know what it is
Do you, Mister Jones?

You hand in your ticket
And you go watch the geek
Who immediately walks up to you
When he hears you speak
And says, "How does it feel to be such a freak?"
And you say, "Impossible", as he hands you a bone
And something is happening here
But you don't know what it is
Do you, Mister Jones?

---

113   Dylan, Bob, Ballad of a Thin Man, on *Highway 61 Revisited*, Columbia, 1965. (With this song, Bob Dylan speaks to the journalists who criticized him in the 1960s. He wrote these lyrics to make fun of their useless job, their pointless questions, and their artistic inadequacy, which drove him up the wall)

You have many contacts among the lumberjacks
To get you facts when someone attacks your imagination
But nobody has any respect
Anyway, they already expect you
To all give a check to tax-deductible charity organizations
Ah, you've been with the professors
And they've all liked your looks
With great lawyers you have discussed lepers and crooks
You've been through all of F. Scott Fitzgerald's books
You're very well read, it's well known
But something is happening here
And you don't know what it is
Do you, Mister Jones?

Well, the sword swallower, he comes up to you
And then he kneels
He crosses himself and then he clicks his high heels
And without further notice he asks you how it feels
And he says, "Here is your throat back, thanks for the loan"
And you know something is happening
But you don't know what it is
Do you, Mister Jones?

Now, you see this one-eyed midget
Shouting the word "Now"
And you say, "For what reason?"
And he says, "How?"
And you say, "What does this mean?"
And he screams back, "You're a cow"
"Give me some milk or else go home"
And you know something's happening
But you don't know what it is
Do you, Mister Jones?

Well, you walk into the room
Like a camel and then you frown
You put your eyes in your pocket
And your nose on the ground
There ought to be a law against you comin' around
You should be made to wear earphones
'Cause something is happening
And you don't know what it is
Do you, Mister Jones?

INTERTEXTUALITY

OVER THE YEARS, critics and artists have accused Bob Dylan of lifting words and phrases from other artists' work and using them as his own, stretching back to the advent of his prolific career and long before the artist delivered his magnificent Nobel Prize speech. But are these allegations true or urban legends?

There is a tremendous difference between being influenced and inspired by a fellow artist's work and picking up words and lines and putting them into one's own songs. Picasso once said about creativity: "Good artist copy. But great artists steal."[114] What Picasso really meant by "steal" is using someone else's work as a starting point and then altering and embellishing it with one's own creative and artistic imprint.

You may not know it, but many creative geniuses—Eliot, Ernest Hemingway, Einstein, and others—have made similar statements. General knowledge, a theoretical and practical understanding of any subject, doesn't land in your lap; you must go out and search for it. And Dylan has gained tremendous knowledge both through reading and through his experiences.

I cannot but agree with Picasso's statement. Let us look at the concept of intertextuality to help clarify the difference between borrowing and plagiarism. "Intertextuality" is attributed to French Bulgarian writer and psychoanalyst Julia Kristeva, a renowned figure in poststructuralist literary theory, which was in full swing in 1960 in Paris, France. Intertextuality is derived from the Latin word *"intertexto,"* which translates as "intermingle while weaving."

Kristeva was the first writer to introduce this specific concept into

---

114   https://creativityclasses.com/good-artists-copy-great-artists-steal/

the study of literature. She claimed that all texts are in conversation with other texts, and they cannot be read or understood in their totality without a proper understating of their interrelatedness.

Intertextuality has to do with a set of associations that are either implicit or explicit in the text or that the reader brings into the reading experience. Intertextuality can emerge from a network of relationships between different texts, whether they are by the same author or not. We often encounter intertextuality because the characteristics that define contemporary literary works relate to experiences, knowledge, writings, and the historical and social background of the given time.

Intertextuality most obviously appears when a work rests on the shoulder of an older literary text, even if that older text is not mentioned at all. A striking example of intertextuality is James Joyce's *Ulysses*, a novel based on the Odyssey. Published on February 2, 1922, Joyce's birthday, it is considered the most important work of modernist literature. Many readers are puzzled, daunted, and amazed by it.

Detecting intertextuality and seeing through a new analytical perspective imbues the text with greater depth, meaning, and substance. The texts might also interact with each other in a way that highlights contrasts, arguments, and new messages. Initially, intertextuality was used as a device to unlock and analyze literary texts; however, it has spread to the fields of advertising and journalism as well.

By studying this phenomenon, you can find that classical texts carry a common Catholic heritage, which the modern writer uses to dust and polish his subject and hold it under the light to discover new truths, secrets, and awakenings.

The Nobel poet laureate Giorgos Seferis said, "Parthenogenesis in art doesn't exist."[115]

Also, it is worth noting that there is no relation between intertextuality and plagiarism. Plagiarism happens when a writer copies someone else's words verbatim without mentioning the originator's

---

115   https://www.tanea.gr/2012/01/20/politics/mikropolitikos/oi-idees-twn-allwn/

name. Intertextuality exists when an author borrows thoughts or phrases from another work and transforms them into something completely new, putting their own soul and heart into it. Two palpable examples are Constantine Cavafy's "Ithaca," a poem dressed musically by Vangelis Papathanassiou and recited by the extraordinary actor Sean Connery on a 2004 CD, and Leonard Cohen's song "Alexandra Leaving," which clearly converses with the poem "The God Abandons Antony," also written by Cavafy.

In conclusion, though analysts and critics continue to find references to other writers in Dylan's work, Dylan is no plagiarist; Dylan's way is authentic and original.

Over a swell dinner and a few glasses of wine, Eliot once said to a good friend of his, "Immature poets imitate. Mature poets steal,"[116] while Hemingway claimed, "It would take a day to list everyone I borrowed ideas from, and it was no new thing for me to learn from everyone I could, living or dead. I learn as much from painters about how to write as I do from writers."[117]

---

116 https://www.goodreads.com/quotes/7832410-immature-poets-imitate-mature-poets-steal-bad-poets-deface-what
117 https://creativityclasses.com/good-artists-copy-great-artists-steal/

CARL JUNG

The Collective Unconscious

IN THE FIRST chapter of the book, we read that director Martin Scorsese shot the documentary *No Direction Home* about the life of the great troubadour. Somewhere toward the end of the first part of the film, Dylan's friend and musician Dave Van Ronk says:[118] "It's almost enough to make you believe in Jung's notion of collective unconscious. If there is such a thing as an American collective unconscious, . . . Bobby had somehow tapped into it."

What did Van Ronk mean with regard to the collective unconscious?

One of the greatest figures of analytical psychology is undoubtedly the Swiss psychologist Carl Jung (1875–1961). From an early age, Jung had extraordinary prophetic dreams and visions, and this was perhaps the main impetus ushering him into the fantastic and mysterious world of psychiatry and psychoanalysis.

He teamed up with Freud at the beginning of his career, and together they discussed, studied, and wrote about the soul and consciousness. But their friendship grew fraught early on; Jung began working on his own scientific and philosophical research that contradicted Freud's theories and practices. After many experiments on his patients, Jung strongly believed that the world needed gods and that no one should try to abolish religions if they had nothing better to replace them with. Christianity, for instance, had soaked the human mind for two thousand years and become part of a historical process that was necessary for the development and evolution

---

118   https://theysaidso.com/quotes/author/dave-van-ronk

of consciousness. He believed that when someone broke away from religion, the metaphysical vacuum created in their soul would destroy them and push them into the world of nihilism.

After traveling extensively and studying the differences and similarities between Indigenous cultures, he brought new attention to the Hermetic tradition, a metaphysical system of divinatory, astrological, and alchemical practices related to the occult teachings of the mythological Hellenistic figure Mercury Trismegistus, a fusion of the Greek god Hermes and the Egyptian god Thoth. What made a big impression on Jung was that similar alchemical symbols were often found in modern dreams and fantasies, and he was certain that at one time the alchemists must have written a manual on the collective unconscious.

Jung went on to develop the concepts of an extroverted and introverted personality, archetypes, and the collective unconscious. As a result, his work has successfully infiltrated both psychiatry and the arts.

For Jung, the collective unconscious mind is a dark, uncharted, and mysterious territory that shelters the memories, emotions, unfulfilled desires and dreams, childhood traumas, and repressed painful thoughts of every human being. As for the personal unconscious, that arises from the experience of the individual.

After years of hard work, Jung realized that within this enigmatic place was a piece of world heritage, something like an a priori source of knowledge planted in every embryo at the time of its conception. He believed that instincts and archetypes are a universal source of wisdom common to all mankind. He writes, "Until you make the unconscious conscious, it will direct your life and you will call it fate."[119] Simply put, the collective unconscious is an invisible inner library filled with ancient experiences that bind humans together—experiences that sneak into dreams, mythology, symbols, and art.

In closing, Jung's work tells us that for anyone who wishes to understand the soul of a human, reading books is insufficient. Instead, we

---

119   https://www.goodreads.com/author/quotes/38285.C_G_Jung

should visit prisons, sanatoriums, hospitals, taverns, brothels, casinos, party gatherings, hospitals, museums, churches, etc. In this way we'll grasp the concept of the soul and understand it better than any persistent scientist hunched over books at his desk for hours on end.

And I believe that Bob Dylan is an artist who has been out and about, who has seen and done things, studied the human mind, heart, and soul, and managed to tap into the world's collective unconscious like no other artist of his generation.

SWEDISH ACADEMY

Talent and Taste.

NOBEL PRIZE

THE SWEDISH ACADEMY was founded by King Gustav III in Stockholm, Sweden, in 1786 as one of Sweden's Royal Academies. Its motto is "Talent and taste." Since 1901, the Academy has decided who will be awarded the highest literary honor in the world, named after the Swedish chemist Alfred Nobel (1833–1896).

Nobel was a distinguished inventor mainly active in the war industry. His most renowned patents are for dynamite and the detonator. A pacifist, he believed that through his work he could put an end to war; however, the media called him the "Merchant of Death."[120] Shortly before he died, he left most of his wealth to establish the Nobel Foundation.

Five years after his death, the Foundation awarded the first Nobel Prizes. The winners were German physicist Wilhelm Roentgen, who discovered X-rays; Dutch chemist Jacobus van Hoff, who formed the laws of chemical dynamics and osmosis of pressure in solutions; the German physician and physiologist Emil von Behring for his work on the diphtheria antitoxin; the French poet and essayist Sully Prudhomme; and finally the Swiss merchant Henrique Dunant and the French Frédéric Passy, who shared the Nobel Peace Prize, the former for the establishment of the Red Cross, and the latter for his work toward international peace.

Right from the beginning, the Nobel Prizes were universally popular, attracting the attention of artists, scientists, and politicians. The Academy initially awarded the disciplines of physics, chemistry, medicine, literature, and peace; a prize in economics was added in 1968. The Nobel Peace Prize is unique among these awards and,

---

120   https://www.thestatesman.com/features/alfred-nobel-from-merchant-of-death-to-pioneer-of-nobel-prize-1503117773.html

according to Alfred's wishes, is given at the city hall of Oslo, Norway.

Previous winners can win again. No one deceased can be nominated. Following author Erik Karlfeldt's win in 1931, no one can be selected as winner posthumously. If someone wins and then passes away before they receive the award, the ceremony still takes place, as was done with pacifist Dag Hammarskjold in 1961 and Dr. Ralph Steinman in 2011; in Steinman's case, the committee was unaware that he had passed away three days before the winner was selected, and the prize remained unchanged.

Nobel laureates win a gold medal, a commemorative diploma, and a check for approximately 900,000 euros. If someone refuses the prize or does not turn up on the day of the ceremony, their name is written on the gold list, but the money, if it is not picked up before the agreed-upon deadline for delivering the Nobel lecture, returns to the funds of the institution.

This happened in 1958 with the writer Boris Pasternak, who was under immense pressure from the communist government of the Soviet Union not to accept the honor. His novel *Doctor Zhivago* was banned in the Soviet Union because it slung arrows at Stalinism. Though Pasternak refused the award, he was still threatened with exile. Finally, in 1989, the Academy gave his Nobel to his son.

French activist, philosopher, and founder of modern existentialism Jean-Paul Sartre—whose work not only speaks of the spirit of freedom, truth, duty, and responsibility but also about the role of man in a meaningless world—decided not to accept the award in 1964. He explained himself in a letter:[121]

> The writer who accepts an honor of this kind involves as well as himself the association or institution which has honored him. The writer must therefore refuse to let himself be transformed into an institution, even if this occurs under the most

---

121 https://www.monopoli.gr/2021/10/22/istories/san-simera/348866/otan-o-zan-pol-sartr-arnithike-to-vraveio-nompel/

honorable circumstances, as in the present case. Moreover, these values also expose the reader to pressure which I don't wish. Signing as Jean-Paul Sartre is not the same as signing as Jean-Paul Sartre, winner of the Nobel.

Although most of the winners of the Nobel Prize in Literature have been men, we must not overlook the seventeen great women who have won: Selma Lagerlöf, Grazia Deledda, Sigrid Undset, Pearl S. Buck, Gabriela Mistral, Nelly Sachs, Nadine Gordimer, Toni Morrison, Wisława Szymborska, Elfriede Jelinek, Doris Lessing, Herta Müller, Alice Monroe, Svetlana Alexievich, Olga Tokarczuk, Louise Glück, and Annie Ernaux.

Unfortunately, the Nobels cannot be awarded to everyone who might deserve them. Many authors of huge influence have never been honored: Jorge Luis Borges, Bertolt Brecht, Anton Chekhov, Umberto Eco, Aldous Huxley, Henry Ibsen, James Joyce, Franz Kafka, Nikos Kazantzakis, Vladimir Nabokov, George Orwell, Fernando Pessoa, Ezra Pound, Marcel Proust, Leo Tolstoy, Mark Twain, Virginia Woolf, Constantine P. Cavafy, Sylvia Plath, Milan Kundera, Vladimir Mayakovsky, Federico García Lorca, and others.

Several American authors have won the Nobel, but the last time the Nobel crossed the Atlantic before Dylan was for Toni Morrison in 1993. Most of the awards have ended up in the hands of the French, British, and Americans, followed by the Germans, Swedes, Spaniards, and Italians.

According to Alfred Nobel's will, a writer should be honored either for the entirety of their work or for their overall contribution to culture and letters. But there are some exceptions. Hemingway was honored specifically for *The Old Man and Sea*, Thomas Mann for *Buddenbrooks: The Decline of a Family*, and Mikhail Sholokhov for the *Harvest on the Don*.

The Academy did not award anybody in 1914, 1918, 1935, or during the Second World War. In 1953, instead of receiving the Nobel

Peace Prize, as many assumed would be the case, Winston Churchill was awarded the Nobel Prize in Literature "for his mastery of historical and biographical description as well as for brilliant oratory in defending exalted human values."

I have come to realize that there is little controversy or reaction regarding the winners in physics, chemistry, and medicine compared to the categories of peace and literature. The latter draw in much more controversy for the fluidity of the concepts they represent.

Greece has won the Nobel Prize in Literature twice, with the poets Giorgos Seferis in 1963 and Odysseus Elytis in 1979. Both poets are known by pseudonyms, as their surnames are Seferiadis and Alepoudelis, respectively.

In 2018, the Swedish Academy decided not to award anybody. Many wondered why. Then the Swedish newspaper *Dagens Nyheter*, along with other international newspapers and magazines, published several sexual harassment complaints against French photographer Jean-Claude Arnault. He is married to the poet Katarina Frostenson, who happened to be a member of the Academy until 2019. Arnault was also accused of other illegal actions, such as leaking the names of Nobel candidates, who have long been subjects of betting pools.

When the above facts came to light, eight of the eighteen members of the Academy resigned, including Frostenson and the institution's secretary, Sarah Danius. The remaining academics decided not to award anybody in the absence of key executives. But they left open the possibility that there would be two awards in 2019.

The last time group resignations made headlines was in 1989 when three academics reacted to an Academy decision not to denounce a fatwa[122] against author Salman Rushdie for his book *The Satanic*

---

122 In February 1989, on Valentine's Day, Iran's religious leader, Ayatollah Khomeini, issued over Radio Tehran a fatwa (religious decree) that asked every faithful Muslim on earth to assassinate Salman Rushdie and the publishers of his book because of blasphemous chapters ridiculing Muhammad and the Koran. This was the first time a spiritual leader had asked such a thing for a citizen of another country.

Verses. The Academy finally denounced the fatwa in 2016. A question that arises is this: as a global proponent of literary prestige, should the Academy immediately take a stand and defend the right to freedom of speech?

To be honest, I believe the Academy hasn't been receiving the best reviews lately; proportionately few of the prizes have been awarded to women and non-Whites, while English-speaking winners are almost twice as numerous as their counterparts from the next most awarded language, French. And the most discouraging fact is that about 90 percent of the prizes are sheltered in European houses. In fact, in 1974 the Academy did not hesitate to award two of its own members, the poets Harry Martinson and Eyvind Johnson. That incident caused a severe international reaction.

When in 1979 the Swedes decided to honor two Greek poets, Odysseus Elytis and Yannis Ritsos, the poets refused to share the prize. The Nobel then went to Elytis for *The Axion Esti*. Rumor has it that Elytis was chosen because his poetry was better suited to the ideology of the Academy and because Ritsos had recently been awarded the prestigious Lenin Prize of the Soviet Union.

Every year, the Academy struggles to choose the five best authors and then honor just one of them. The problem is that no one knows the criteria by which one candidate wins the prize and how objective the committee is—after all, the meetings remain top secret for the next fifty years. Lately, the Nobel Foundation has accused the Academy of a lack of transparency, and the Academy has promised that changes will be made soon. My guess is that the Foundation will suggest putting an end to the lifelong position the Academy's members hold so that the institution, which has increasingly lost its glow, can become more transparent and fairer.

In October 2019, after a difficult period wherein the institution lost some of its dignity and prestige, the new secretary of the institution, writer and professor Mats Malm, announced two winners: the Polish writer Olga Tokarczuk in 2018 "for a narrative imagination that with encyclopedic passion represents the crossing of boundaries as a form of life," and the Austrian writer Peter Handke in 2019 "for an influential work that with linguistic ingenuity has explored the periphery and the specificity of human experience."

A TRADITION THAT BEGINS WITH HOMER

As we have seen, the Swedish Academy considers Bob Dylan to be the heir to a long oral tradition beginning with Homer and Sappho. But what did Sarah Danius mean by this?

To provide a satisfying answer and a clear picture, I have divided known history into three main periods: antiquity, the Middle Ages, and the modern age. Working backward, we'll begin with the distinguished and dark personality of poet Ezra Pound, who contributed a great deal to the development and formation of modernism.

Ezra Pound (1885–1972)

Together with Nobel laureate T. S. Eliot, the American poet Ezra Pound is considered one of the main representatives of literary modernism. Eliot admired the boundless and complex meanings of Pound's style and in his notes called him "*il miglior fabbro*," i.e., "the great craftsman."[123]

Pound was fascinated with the literature of the East and with the Chinese ideograms that harmoniously marry visual works of art with the textual. Engaged in imagism—a movement originating in the classical poetry of China, which focuses on precision and economy of language—Pound also loved the theater genre Noh, Japanese drama accompanied by a choir and music reminiscent of opera.

At the beginning of the twentieth century, Pound traveled to London, where he worked as a correspondent for American

---

123 https://dualpersonalities.wordpress.com/2022/10/24/il-miglior-fabbro/

newspapers. His writing influenced the work of contemporary writers such as Joyce and Hemingway; and Seferis, who listened to cantos I, XIII, and XLIX on the radio in 1959, was mesmerized by Pound's strong, rhythmic, and gentle voice. A few years later, Seferis translated the first two cantos into the Greek language.

Disturbed by the death and squalor of WWI, Pound left England and moved to Italy. There, he grew disturbed at the practice of money-lending and at capitalism spreading like gangrene. Thus, in the 1930s he sided with Mussolini, supported Hitler, and published articles in fascist newspapers. During WWII, as a radio producer he was paid by the Italian government to criticize President Roosevelt and the Jews.

When the war ended, American soldiers arrested him for treason and put him in solitary confinement in an uncovered barbed-wire cage in the city of Pisa. Then they shipped him to America, where a judge concluded that Pound could not stand trial because he was mentally and spiritually unfit. Pound was put in a mental institution in Washington, DC.

While in Pisa, he worked on *The Cantos* and published the long and incomplete poem under the title *The Pisan Cantos* in 1948. In this work, we can trace an element of contemplation concerning not only his personal downfall and his moral decline but also the destruction of Europe on all levels. In 1949, Pound was awarded the Bollingen Prize. In 1958, he returned to Italy, where he lived until his death in Venice in 1972.

His views on politics remained ambiguous and dark, while his attitude toward WWII is a good subject for discussion on whether we should judge an artist for his work or based on his ideologies. Many translators, literary critics, artists, writers, and readers are torn between hate and love for his work. *Time* magazine describes him as a cat that walks by himself, tenaciously unhousebroken and very unsafe for children, whereas Hemingway said that Pound's best writing would last as long as literature exists.[124]

---

124   https://forreadingaddicts.co.uk/poetry/the-controversy-of-ezra-pound/

Pound considered the relationship between poetry and music ideal and urged his peers to write with the intention that their poems be sung and transmitted through the melodious air of the human voice. He argued that the separation of these two arts flourished mainly in times of moral decay.

Let us briefly consider the main differences between Pound and Eliot. Some think that Pound failed to complete his grandiose and poetic vision. I don't know if this is the case, but it is a fact that good and "successful" poetry is usually written by writers like Eliot, on the grounds that they avoid wrestling with contentious issues. Especially if you are talented, like Eliot, and deal with simple, everyday issues, it is easier to write perfect poetry. Some argue that though Eliot's work is great, it cannot move you the way *The Cantos* can. And I believe *The Cantos* have incomparable emotional and spiritual energy and dynamism because the poet completed them while isolated with his thoughts and regrets in Pisa.

Ezra Pound was a giant of a poet, but unlike Eliot, he never won the Nobel Prize in Literature, mostly due to his unacceptable political beliefs.

But let's continue our beautiful journey through time, approaching the Middle Ages and then antiquity. As I have already said, Pound recommended that universities teaching philology and literature hire singers, since he believed that only through melody would the student feel the soul and heart of poetry. Cantos are "songs," and in them he mentions the names of troubadours of Provence.

The great troubadours of the late Middle Ages established the model of the artist writing metered poetic lines, setting them to music, and then singing while playing the lute or harp. The famous singers of Provence usually praised Platonic love and were a source of inspiration for Dante Alighieri when he wrote *Paradise*, the third book of the *Divine Comedy*, a work of unsurpassed beauty and power that has undoubtedly influenced Western literature and thought to this day.

The Troubadours of Provence

From the eleventh to the thirteenth century, literature flourished mainly in the courts of European nobility and was divided into three main categories: epic, novel, and lyric poetry.

This was when the troubadours appeared in Provence. They did not write in Latin, as was customary, but rather in a language that no longer exists. Their dialect was called *langue d'óc*, or Occitan, and is considered one of the first historically significant languages of European world literature. This language took its name from the affirmative particle "óc" ("yes") and was spoken and sung in the regions of Provence in France before migrating to Italy and Spain.

The word "troubadour" comes from "*trobar*," which means "to find or invent" in the sense of composing. Troubadours or wandering artists helped spread folk traditions from place to place without recording their poetry and music. As a result, their work existed only in memories and in their living traditions. At the end of the thirteenth century, grammarians and scholars took the vastly important step of collecting and recording the wonderful poems of troubadours. This act has helped us to investigate the worldview of the poets of Occitania and to understand why and how they paved the way for future generations.

Their Provençal lyricism began with Homer, Hesiod, and Sappho and ended with Beatrice in the *Divine Comedy* by Dante. With gentle courtesy and respect, they glorified love for women, which was related to Christianity and the Virgin Mary. In a sense, Platonic love elevated women into angelic creatures, as happened in the myths of Lancelot and Guinevere. Little by little, this approach to art created a chivalric ideal that set aside the wretchedness of power, which saw, considered, and treated woman as inferior to and as the property of man.

Their songs carried symbolic confessions mirroring the divine relationship between man and nature, and it is worth noting that this adherence to Platonic love softened people's mistrust of the church, which at times expressed opposition to these love songs.

The basic characteristics of the troubadours' art that distinguished it from the rest of medieval literature are as follows: first, they composed short poems in everyday language (Òc) rather than Latin. And second, they spontaneously followed their inspiration and narrated subjective feelings. The moral these itinerant travelers represented was growth and the improvement of the spirit and soul through the search for a personal lost paradise.

Their music and songs had a melodic line repeated in every stanza, and their instruments were mainly stringed, such as the lute and the harp. The most dominant musical form of the thirteenth century was the motet, which evolved from the troubadours but added other notes, resulting in a newer and freer form of polyphony.

The famous troubadours of the Middle Ages no longer exist. But their aura and spirit remains and lives in the subconscious of every person who today decides to sit down and write a song.

Ancient Greece and Poetry

In ancient Greece, when someone talked about poetry, they were typically referring to a musical event. The Homeric epics, for example, contain rhapsodies that were usually recited to the accompaniment of the lyre, expressing the ideals of the time as they glorified heroes and brave warriors. Something similar applies to the choruses of tragedies, which consist of metered verses set to music. In the theater of the time, dance was not just a circle of people making pantomime gestures; they also sang. Like epics, choral poetry was written to address a live audience.

In the seventh century BC, Sappho, the famous lyric poet from Lesvos, was interested in music, and she usually incorporated it into rituals and worship of the gods. In several surviving pieces from her work, you can clearly see that the melody contributes to the educational sculpting of human character, spirit, and soul.

The Homeric epics made another appearance during the European Renaissance, a period of recovery for the arts and letters where poetry, music, and orchesis (representation) became important. Even today, the drama of the ancient Greeks is considered one of the most important and sublime forms of expression in its combination of three basic elements: speech, melody, and movement, which in turn touch the spirit, soul, and body. According to many scholars, the secret of this success is hidden in the rhythm, which does not exist in text alone or even in sound but rather in combination with representation. Ancient Greek poetry was heard and watched as a spectacle. In other words, it was oral.

In ancient Greece, music without a voice was unimaginable. The ancient philosophers considered organic music a subordinate genre and decided not to give it a name. They just called it craft, which nowadays we typically use to refer to the work of artisans engaged in manual work. The element of imitation is something only words can accurately achieve. A sound without text is abstract, vague, and undefined because it remains permanently open to multiple subjective interpretations. Thus, it is considered suspect. The job of a proper musical piece is to express meaning, to refer to the muses and to gods and to problems and worries of the time.

In order to understand the concept of imitation better, I would like us to consider the following. Suppose one composer wishes to convey to his audience a specific image, e.g., a battlefield, a house on the prairie, or a galloping horse. How can he, without speech, create images of geometric clarity and mathematical precision?

I'm afraid he cannot. Though music has its own language, it can only convey abstract feelings, not concrete pictures and meanings. According to the view of the ancient Greeks, music can imitate virtue, mercy, and goodness only if it has within its essence the word—that is, poetry.

When Plato, the philosopher who laid the unshakable foundations for the Western way of thinking and perception, talked about music, he always meant text accompanied by a melody. These two artistic and creative elements, together with body language, transcend the soul and the spirit and bring us to higher mental planes. Meanwhile, the musicians kept a distance from the text, for they wanted to present their skill and improvisational abilities freed from the constraints and commitments poetry requires. Plato did not hold these talented musicians in high esteem; they did not try to project the moral standards that a given verse contained, and they flirted with a cocky projection of the self.

In his masterpiece *The Symposium*, where the philosopher explores love, he seems to want to downgrade music as mere entertainment, believing that it cannot reach the spiritual and emotional level that the conversation between the guests in his work manages to reach. He tells us that no musician worth his salt does not put poetry in his work, which in turn must offer correct political, social, cultural, and artistic standards to the people of the particular era.

The educational system of ancient Greece was straightforward. The music course involved singing, playing an instrument, and dancing. It also taught the art of recitation and lyrical poems, always accompanied by the lyre.

By observing the young people, Plato realized that the uneducated ones acted more out of emotion than reason. Therefore, he concluded that works presenting negative patterns of behavior (e.g., *Medea*), behaviors capable of emotionally fueling the young and leading them to indecent and evil actions, must be thrown out of the pedagogical system.

On the other hand, Plato's student, the inexhaustible philosopher Aristotle, tells us in *Poetics*, the first creative writing book in the world, that epic poetry and the poetry of tragedy belong to the arts that imitate rhythm, speech, and melody, while the art that imitates with speech alone, either in prose or just with lyrics, is anonymous, incomplete, and immature.

Comedy and tragedy, those two ubiquitous genres of human expression through which man analyzes and searches for his lost self, began with improvisations linked to dithyrambs and Dionysian songs, respectively. Tragedies typically consist of six main elements: myth (plot), morals (characters), style (words), intellect (thought), appearance (spectacular elements of the performance), and composition (music), which is considered to be the main flavoring of a play.

Aristotle believed that society consisted of excellent citizens and that the rest—farmers, professionals, merchants, and slaves—did not possess the luxury of virtuous behavior. In this case, it would be normal for two kinds of music to appear. On the one side would be the music addressed to the cultured and on the other side the music that entertains the rest. The philosopher concluded that each listener, depending on their level of knowledge, would prefer to listen to music matching their psyche. Therefore, it was useless to try, like Plato, to educate all citizens by imposing an extreme and absolute way.

On the strength of what the two great philosophers have said, I would like to explain my own way of thinking. I believe that the perfect balance is found between two extremes—what is often referred to as the "golden mean." Aristotle analyzes the golden mean in *Nicomachean Ethics Book II*. In the Aristotelian view, courage is a virtue, but if a person takes it to its extreme, it becomes recklessness; in deficiency, it becomes cowardice. In our four-dimensional world, we perceive reality as a balance of positive and negative qualities. If we want to experience true happiness, first we must experience true sadness; if we want to experience true love, we must experience hate; if we want to experience true bravery, we must experience true fear, and so on and so forth.

Now, if we want to help a person reach their potential through a proper academic and liberal education, we must try to inject in them, through the arts, both positive and negative elements in equal dosages. Anyone who experiences only beautiful things in life, as

Plato recommends, will become meek, weak, and afraid when negative aspects of reality come their way. They will not be able to face and fight them. Thus, in my humble opinion, if we want to create a balanced psyche, people must experience both extremes. In that way, we will hopefully strike a balance.

∼

Friedrich Nietzsche (1844–1900)

Let us bounce forward again to another enlightened philosopher, Friedrich Nietzsche (1844–1900). In his book *The Birth of Tragedy*, he tells us that a man can only succeed in regenerating civilization by bringing to stage the tragic element through which a balanced and harmonious coexistence is created between Dionysus, the god of drunkenness and orgies, and Apollo, the god of measure and beauty. The Apollonian ideology is considered the principle of individuation, restraint, and modesty, while the Dionysian ideology values excess.

The Dionysian element initially appeared in the barbarians who roamed the steppes before the rise of Greek civilization. Its main characteristics are drunkenness and orgies. Through drunkenness, a man frees himself from rigid and hard logic and enters the world of desire, where he can plunge into unbridled pleasures that feed and satisfy his passions. In the early Greek world of Homer and Hesiod, the Apollonian element dominated and the plastic arts flourished. But mysticism, magic, and the religious element of worship also permeated Greece. Ceremonies accompanied by wine were at their zenith and reflected the triumph of will and a zest for life. The Dionysian element is a cry of the heart that seeks extravagance, pleasure, and liberation, wanting to forget and escape Apollonian measures, limitations, and boundaries. And when exaggeration occurs, it is understood as truth. Thus, Nietzsche considered the Dionysian element the basic precondition of people's songs.

In the fifth century BC, at the height of Greek civilization, the Apollonian and the Dionysian elements united. The result of this marriage was the birth of tragedy and an interesting union of music and dance. Music and dance, according to Nietzsche, express the rhythm of not only primal being but also chaos and the abyss. Nietzsche considered tragedy to be the highest creation of ancient Greek art because it unified two gods who were in a constant struggle.

So, tragedy was born through the spirit of music. The differences between people, the gaps between state and society, collapsed in the face of an overpowering feeling of unity, which led people straight back to the heart of nature. With the dynamics of music, the listeners remain fixated on illusions that help them enter the magical world of myths expressed in tragedies.

NOBEL PRIZE WINNERS

Now, it's time to get off the magic bus to times past and return to frozen Scandinavia and the Swedish Academy.

When then secretary of the institution Sarah Danius announced to her audience that the winner of the 2016 Nobel Prize in Literature was a singer, a reporter raised his hand and asked, "Have you expanded the boundaries of literature?"

But what did this man mean? He apparently believed that only literary poetry and prose were worthy of the Nobel Prize and anything different should be considered beyond the bounds of the contest or as something totally new. But was this the way things stood?

At this point, I would like to shed light on two past winners: the journalist Svetlana Alexievich (2015) and the playwright Dario Fo (1997). These two winners certainly did not write classic literature. The former created a new genre known now as prose of testimony, while the latter staged theatrical performances based on improvisation and a kind of metalanguage influenced by commedia dell'arte of the sixteenth century.

So, I think we are ready to reply to the journalist that the boundaries of literature didn't suddenly open and expand with Bob Dylan; they had been opened as far back as 1913 when Indian poet Rabindranath Tagore won the Nobel for writing songs and hymns for many countries around the world.

Let us now delve into the particulars of the matter at hand and try to understand what all the above really means. Then we will take a look at the long list of artists who have won the Nobel since 1901 and why they won it.

Svetlana Alexievich (1948–)

Raised in Belarus, Svetlana Alexievich is a Ukrainian investigative journalist, essayist, and historian. In 2015 she won the Nobel Prize in Literature for her polyphonic writings, a monument to suffering and courage in our time. In her writings, she narrates World War II, the Soviet invasion of Afghanistan, the fall of the USSR, and the consequences of the Chernobyl nuclear accident through eyewitnesses and manages to give a new perspective to journalism.

Her first book, *The Unwomanly Face of War: An Oral History of Women in World War II*, shares accounts of women fighting in the war, while in her second book, *Last Witnesses: An Oral History of Children in World War II*, various adults discuss their childhood memories from the same war. *Zinky Boys: Soviet Voices from the Afghanistan War*, published in 1989, reveals the truth about the Soviet war in Afghanistan, which had been ongoing for almost a decade. The book has been banned in Belarus and caused strong reactions in the military establishment and the Soviet regime. Although Svetlana faced many court trials, she proceeded with her head held high, and in 1993, her book *Fascinated by Death* focused on the countless suicides in the former Soviet Union after the collapse of communism.

Four years later, *Voices from Chernobyl: The Oral History of a Nuclear Disaster* hit the bookstores, incorporating testimonials from the nuclear accident of 1986, which Svetlana diligently collected by wandering through the forbidden zone, risking her own health and life.

"During the ten years I was visiting the Chernobyl zone, I had the impression that I was recording the future,"[125] Alexievich tells us, completing her literary masterpiece redefining the concept of evidence in literature.

Her writing confirms the words of the Jewish author Elie Wiesel: "The twentieth century is the testimony century or otherwise of the

---

125 https://www.dalkeyarchive.com/2013/08/02/a-conversation-with-svetlana-alexievich-by-ana-lucic/

voices of anonymous people that were victims of the historical events that undermined the values of our civilization to the fullest through inhuman events such as the holocaust, gulags, warfare against civilians and ecological disasters."[126]

Svetlana Alexievich won the Nobel Prize in Literature because she presents events in a way that brings a different perspective to our eyes. Her work makes us appreciate life and try to be better human beings. These testimonies become universal life myths.

I would like to present a chilling passage from the book *Chernobyl Prayer: A Chronicle of the Future* that reminds us of the past and warns us about the future. The book shows what it feels like to be a witness to such a terrible disaster and remember all of it in a world that wants you to forget.

> In the winter the cats were so hungry that they ate their kittens. Forgive me, my God! The rats ate an old woman. Red rats. I don't know if it's true but that's what they told me. The area is filled with homeless people who came here to steal. At first, they found many things in the houses. Shirts, sweaters, and even furs. They took and sold them in the bazaars. They were getting drunk, swearing, and singing. One night, one of them fell from the bicycle and fell asleep on the road. The next morning, they found only his bones. True or false, I don't know. So they say, at least.[127]

∼

Dario Fo (1926–2016)

The multidimensional, versatile, and avant-garde Italian playwright, actor, and director Dario Fo was socially and politically acidic

---

126 https://www.elenifourli.gr/36-chronia-apo-dystychima-sto-tsernompil-o-kosmos-thymatai-kai-anisychei/

127 Alexievich, Svetlana, *Chernobyl – A chronicle of the Future*, Patakis-Greek Publications, 2015, p. 67.

and subversive. Dario learned the art of storytelling from his grandmother and from Lombard fishermen, and in 1997 he won the Nobel Prize in Literature.

During World War II, he and his family took part in the antifascist resistance, fleeing to Switzerland. After 1945, Fo continued the architectural studies he began in Milan before the war. At night, in small theaters and cabarets, he performed monologues based mostly on improvisation in which he verbally eviscerated power, giving back to the humble their lost respect and vigor.

In 1969, he presented to the public *Mistero Buffo*, a theatrical monologue combining medieval plays and contemporary problems of his hometown. The performances exceeded five thousand iterations, and several were even performed in stadiums. With *Mistero Buffo*, Fo the clown reintroduced narrative theater, a genre similar to the folktale, in which there are no actors who play specific or rehearsed dramatic roles.

A year later, Fo wrote *Accidental Death of an Anarchist* after a far-right terrorist attack on a national agricultural bank in Milan. *Can't Pay? Won't Pay!* from 1974 is a prank of a play where women and men grab whatever they want from the market and make off with the goods.

Through his work, Fo tackled the Catholic church, political assassinations, organized crime, corruption, and problems in the Middle East. He invented linguistic idioms, gestures, and facial expressions in order to pass hidden messages against the existing authority. This hidden language stemmed from sixteenth-century commedia dell'arte.

The metalanguage he used to hide the messages he wanted to pass on to his audience brought enormous problems to his doorstep. He was imprisoned, and his wife and partner, Franca Rame, was kidnapped by fascists, tortured, and raped. But the wounded Dario Fo didn't give up. Through theater, television, and books, he continued to provoke by attacking every form of power, making it not only seem easy and approachable but also funny and inferior to the given circumstances.

It was rumored that he had been honored him with the Nobel because of his hardships. Others said he was recognized for his innovative artistry and value, while the church claimed the Academy's choice revealed the fall in morals and human values. At any rate, because Fo's plays rely heavily on improvisation and body movements, his work ventures far from the static form of a book. This tireless and intelligent artist always encouraged his translators and directors to adapt his texts as they saw fit because he knew that freedom of expression suited the tradition of improvisation begun by commedia dell'arte. His plays are meant to be performed rather than read.

He wrote approximately eighty plays, including *Archangels Don't Play Pinball*; *All House, Bed and Church*; *The Open Couple—Wide Open Even*; *The Pope and the Witch*; *The Devil with Boobs*; and *The Two-Headed Anomaly*. Dario Fo's most talked-about appearance remained his solo role of the clown in *Mistero Buffo*.

His work might have been influenced by medieval mysteries, but its content dealt with the concerns and problems of the area and time his audience lived in.

∼

Commedia dell'Arte

This art of Italian origin refers to folk comedy based on improvisation rather than written words. It developed and became famous from the sixteenth to the eighteenth centuries and was embraced in many parts of Europe.

Commedia dell'arte means "the comedy of art," not with an amateur approach but with a professional concept and technical training. It was primarily created by professional artists and actors rather than amateurs of verbal comedy. These gifted actors not only performed but also created the costumes, masks, and particularities of voice and body language. When dancing, everyone needed physical and mental strength, ability, and flexibility.

This was one of the first theater genres to use female actors, significantly influencing the evolution of theater. The improvisational comedy troupes were itinerant, often using a painted cloth hung at the back of the tent, which they set up in squares or courtyards of mansions. At first, their dialogues were simple, just small talk between two actors, but later they presented plays involving a plot and a larger number of actors, leaning on a basic script or thematic skeleton so as to keep the actors within certain limits, but always maintaining a sense of improvisation.

The actors of the commedia dell'arte had some standard quick jokes with caustic undertones: the famous *consetti*, or verbal jokes. There were also *lazzi*, optical tricks used depending on the occasion; and *burles*, longer stories with more complete humor.

Using the three elements of *consetti*, *lazzi*, and *burle*, while the actors deviated from the basic script, they always returned to the central theme so that the show proceeded and ended normally. They achieved this kind of performance with the great ease of consummate professionals. It helped that they gave countless performances, always playing the same role. Only on special occasions would an actor step into the role of a different character.

Usually, the subject matter involved amorous adventures enriched with topical satire concerning real people and the use of local dialects with corrupt pronunciation. There were often conflicts between opposites: for instance, between cunning and stupidity, master and slave, or thief and policeman.

The roles were stereotyped and mainly divided into three major categories: the wicked servants, the masters, and the lovers. The classic characters of commedia dell'arte are Harlequin, Colombina, Pantalone, Pierrot, Capitano, Dottore, and Brighella.

In closing, commedia dell'arte established representational movement as an international language of expression upon which leading actors such as Charlie Chaplin learned to create their own works of art.

∼

Metalanguage

In the field of metalinguistics, metalanguage refers to the words, phrases, terms, signs, and symbols we use to describe and analyze language itself. In other words, metalanguage is the language used to talk about language.

A simple example is the following: if a literature teacher says to the father of one of his students, "She is a master at writing short stories," the "she" is a personal feminine pronoun, "is" is a form of the verb "to be," "master" is a noun, "at" is a preposition, "writing" is a gerund, and so on and so forth.

There is also a kind of theatrical metalanguage based primarily on body movements and facial expressions, aiming to interpret and explain the actual language. This is a valuable device for theater and acting in general.

Let's go back to the Nobel laureate Dario Fo. We have learned that he liked to create art based on improvisation and by using theatrical metalanguage. Try to picture Fo and some other actors performing on stage. Fo says, "This politician is congenial and has good intentions." As soon as he finishes his sentence, he sends a side-glance to another actor, waggling his eyebrows. Then, he shifts his eyes to another actor, who is presenting an obscene gesture, and a third, who purses and bites his lips.

All this belongs to the realm of theater metalanguage.

～

Rabindranath Tagore (1861–1941)

When the Nobel Prize in Literature ended up in the hands of Bob Dylan, the *New York Times* wrote that it was the first time a musician had been honored.[128] But this statement was far untrue; in 1913,

---

128   https://www.nytimes.com/2016/10/14/arts/music/bob-dylan-nobel-prize-literature.html?fbclid=IwAR1acKDAoJ3WRZGnMvt_1TJIsZlVpUexFTESiuOyfN-1VHRO8aMtEkbJx5DU

another composer, poet, and philosopher won the same award. His name was Rabindranath Tagore.

Born in Calcutta, India, Tagore grew up in a family of artists who fought for a better position for women in Indian society. Tagore wrote more than two thousand songs and poems, some of which were used in Asian films; others are related to ethnic anthems of India, Bangladesh, and Sri Lanka.

Pound compared him to Dante, while Thomas Mann, George Bernard Shaw, and André Gide praised him as one of the best songwriters and poets of the nineteenth century. Some even believed that Tagore's work inspired Pablo Neruda and Octavio Paz. The Swedish Academy singled out his most important work, *Song Offerings* (*Gitanjali* in its original Bengali). Let us have a taste of his poem "The Gardener":[129]

> Who are you, reader, reading my poems hundred years hence?
> I cannot send you one single flower from this wealth of the spring, one single streak of gold from yonder clouds.
> Open your doors and look abroad.
> From your blossoming garden gather fragrant memories of all vanished flowers of a hundred years before.
> In the joy of your heart may you feel the living joy that sang one spring morning, sending its glad voice across a hundred years.

Two years after the Stockholm prize, Tagore was knighted by King George of England, but he gave back the title in 1919 in protest of the massacre of innocents in the city of Amritsar by British forces.

The relationship between Tagore and Dylan reveals clear similarities: both are considered musical poets. But naturally, there are also differences. The American bard won the Nobel "for having created new poetic expressions within the great American song tradition," while Tagore won the Nobel for translating his poetic thoughts into English in a way that made his work part of the West's literary tradition.

---
129   https://www.gutenberg.org/files/6686/6686-h/6686-h.htm

In "Gitanjali 103"[130] he tells us,

> In one salutation to thee, my God, let all my senses spread out and touch this world at thy feet.
>
> Like a rain-cloud of July hung low with its burden of unshed showers let all my mind bend down at thy door in one salutation to thee.
>
> Let all my songs gather together their diverse strains into a single current and flow to a sea of silence in one salutation to thee.
>
> Like a flock of homesick cranes flying night and day back to their mountain nests let all my life take its voyage to its eternal home in one salutation to thee.

Interestingly, modern American composer and pianist Philip Glass, in the "Portrait Trilogy," which was inspired by personalities who changed the world, included Tagore in the second part of the trilogy, entitled *Satyagraha*. Glass dedicated it to Gandhi. In his work, he presents the experiences of the Indian leader who publicly protested the injustices done to people of color in South Africa. The title *Satyagraha* is a Sanskrit word referring to the power of truth, and the opera focuses on Gandhi's ideology of passive resistance against injustice. The seminarrative form is dominated by three historical personalities whose spirits are respectively embodied in the three acts: first Tolstoy, then Tagore, and finally Martin Luther King Jr.

---

130   https://poets.org/poem/gitanjali-103

ALL NOBEL PRIZES IN LITERATURE TO 2020[131]

2020 Louise Glück "for her unmistakable poetic voice that with austere beauty makes individual existence universal."

2019 Peter Handke "for an influential work that with linguistic ingenuity has explored the periphery and the specificity of human experience."

2018 Olga Tokarczuk "for a narrative imagination that with encyclopedic passion represents the crossing of boundaries as a form of life."

2017 Kazuo Ishiguro, "who, in novels of great emotional force, has uncovered the abyss beneath our illusory sense of connection with the world."

2016 Bob Dylan "for having created new poetic expressions within the great American song tradition."

2015 Svetlana Alexievich "for her polyphonic writings, a monument to suffering and courage in our time."

2014 Patrick Modiano "for the art of memory with which he has evoked the most ungraspable human destinies and uncovered the life-world of the occupation."

2013 Alice Munro, "master of the contemporary short story."

2012 Mo Yan, "who with hallucinatory realism merges folk tales, history and the contemporary."

2011 Tomas Tranströmer "because, through his condensed, translucent images, he gives us fresh access to reality."

2010 Mario Vargas Llosa "for his cartography of structures of power and his trenchant images of the individual's resistance, revolt, and defeat."

2009 Herta Müller, "who, with the concentration of poetry and the

---

131   https://www.svenskaakademien.se/en/the-nobel-prize-in-literature/the-laureates

frankness of prose, depicts the landscape of the dispossessed."

2008 Jean-Marie Gustave Le Clézio, "author of new departures, poetic adventure and sensual ecstasy, explorer of a humanity beyond and below the reigning civilization."

2007 Doris Lessing, "that epicist of the female experience, who with scepticism, fire and visionary power has subjected a divided civilisation to scrutiny."

2006 Orhan Pamuk, "who in the quest for the melancholic soul of his native city has discovered new symbols for the clash and interlacing of cultures."

2005 Harold Pinter, "who in his plays uncovers the precipice under everyday prattle and forces entry into oppression's closed rooms."

2004 Elfriede Jelinek "for her musical flow of voices and counter-voices in novels and plays that with extraordinary linguistic zeal reveal the absurdity of society's clichés and their subjugating power."

2003 John M. Coetzee, "who in innumerable guises portrays the surprising involvement of the outsider."

2002 Imre Kertész "for writing that upholds the fragile experience of the individual against the barbaric arbitrariness of history."

2001 Sir Vidiadhar Surajprasad Naipaul "for having united perceptive narrative and incorruptible scrutiny in works that compel us to see the presence of suppressed histories."

2000 Gao Xingjian "for an oeuvre of universal validity, bitter insights and linguistic ingenuity, which has opened new paths for the Chinese novel and drama."

1999 Günter Grass, "whose frolicsome black fables portray the forgotten face of history."

1998 José Saramago, "who with parables sustained by imagination, compassion and irony continually enables us once again to apprehend an elusory reality."

1997 Dario Fo, "who emulates the jesters of the Middle Ages in scourging authority and upholding the dignity of the downtrodden."

1996 Wislawa Szymborska "for poetry that with ironic precision allows the historical and biological context to come to light in fragments of human reality."

1995 Seamus Heaney "for works of lyrical beauty and ethical depth, which exalt everyday miracles and the living past."

1994 Kenzaburo Oe, "who with poetic force creates an imagined world, where life and myth condense to form a disconcerting picture of the human predicament today."

1993 Toni Morrison, "who in novels characterized by visionary force and poetic import, gives life to an essential aspect of American reality."

1992 Derek Walcott "for a poetic oeuvre of great luminosity, sustained by a historical vision, the outcome of a multicultural commitment."

1991 Nadine Gordimer, "who through her magnificent epic writing has—in the words of Alfred Nobel—been of very great benefit to humanity."

1990 Octavio Paz "for impassioned writing with wide horizons, characterized by sensuous intelligence and humanistic integrity."

1989 Camilo José Cela "for a rich and intensive prose, which with restrained compassion forms a challenging vision of man's vulnerability."

1988 Naguib Mahfouz, "who, through works rich in nuance—now clear-sightedly realistic, now evocatively ambiguous—has formed an Arabian narrative art that applies to all mankind."

1987 Joseph Brodsky "for an all-embracing authorship, imbued with clarity of thought and poetic intensity."

1986 Wole Soyinka, "who in a wide cultural perspective and with poetic overtones fashions the drama of existence."

1985 Claude Simon, "who in his novel combines the poet's and the painter's creativeness with a deepened awareness of time in the depiction of the human condition."

1984 Jaroslav Seifert "for his poetry which endowed with freshness, sensuality and rich inventiveness provides a liberating image of the indomitable spirit and versatility of man."

1983 William Golding "for his novels which, with the perspicuity of realistic narrative art and the diversity and universality of myth, illuminate the human condition in the world of today."

1982 Gabriel García Márquez "for his novels and short stories, in which the fantastic and the realistic are combined in a richly composed world of imagination, reflecting a continent's life and conflicts."

1981 Elias Canetti "for writings marked by a broad outlook, a wealth of ideas and artistic power."

1980 Czeslaw Milosz, "who with uncompromising clear-sightedness voices man's exposed condition in a world of severe conflicts."

1979 Odysseus Elytis "for his poetry, which, against the background of Greek tradition, depicts with sensuous strength and intellectual clear-sightedness modern man's struggle for freedom and creativeness."

1978 Isaac Bashevis Singer "for his impassioned narrative art which, with roots in a Polish-Jewish cultural tradition, brings universal human conditions to life."

1977 Vicente Aleixandre "for a creative poetic writing which illuminates man's condition in the cosmos and in present-day society, at the same time representing the great renewal of the traditions of Spanish poetry between the wars."

1976 Saul Bellow "for the human understanding and subtle analysis of contemporary culture that are combined in his work."

1975 Eugenio Montale "for his distinctive poetry which, with great artistic sensitivity, has interpreted human values under the sign of an outlook on life with no illusions"

1974 Eyvind Johnson "for a narrative art, far-seeing in lands and ages, in the service of freedom."

1974 Harry Martinson "for writings that catch the dewdrop and reflect the cosmos."

1973 Patrick White "for an epic and psychological narrative art which has introduced a new continent into literature."

1972 Heinrich Böll "for his writing which through its combination of a broad perspective on his time and a sensitive skill in characterization has contributed to a renewal of German literature."

1971 Pablo Neruda "for a poetry that with the action of an elemental force brings alive a continent's destiny and dreams."

1970 Aleksandr Isayevich Solzhenitsyn "for the ethical force with which he has pursued the indispensable traditions of Russian literature."

1969 Samuel Beckett "for his writing, which—in new forms for the novel and drama—in the destitution of modern man acquires its elevation."

1968 Yasunari Kawabata "for his narrative mastery, which with great sensibility expresses the essence of the Japanese mind."

1967 Miguel Angel Asturias "for his vivid literary achievement, deep-rooted in the national traits and traditions of Indian peoples of Latin America."

1966 Shmuel Yosef Agnon "for his profoundly characteristic narrative art with motifs from the life of the Jewish people."

1966 Nelly Sachs "for her outstanding lyrical and dramatic writing, which interprets Israel's destiny with touching strength."

1965 Mikhail Aleksandrovich Sholokhov "for the artistic power and integrity with which, in his epic of the Don, he has given expression to a historic phase in the life of the Russian people."

1964 Jean-Paul Sartre "for his work which, rich in ideas and filled with the spirit of freedom and the quest for truth, has exerted a far-reaching influence on our age."

1963 Giorgos Seferis "for his eminent lyrical writing, inspired by a deep feeling for the Hellenic world of culture."

1962 John Steinbeck "for his realistic and imaginative writings, combining as they do sympathetic humour and keen social perception."

1961 Ivo Andric "for the epic force with which he has traced themes and depicted human destinies drawn from the history of his country."

1960 Saint-John Perse "for the soaring flight and the evocative imagery of his poetry which in a visionary fashion reflects the conditions of our time."

1959 Salvatore Quasimodo "for his lyrical poetry, which with classical fire expresses the tragic experience of life in our own times."

1958 Boris Leonidovich Pasternak "for his important achievement both in contemporary lyrical poetry and in the field of the great Russian epic tradition."

1957 Albert Camus "for his important literary production, which with clear-sighted earnestness illuminates the problems of the human conscience in our times."

1956 Juan Ramón Jiménez "for his lyrical poetry, which in Spanish language constitutes an example of high spirit and artistical purity"

1955 Halldór Kiljan Laxness "for his vivid epic power which has renewed the great narrative art of Iceland."

1954 Ernest Miller Hemingway "for his mastery of the art of narrative, most recently demonstrated in *The Old Man and the Sea*, and for the influence that he has exerted on contemporary style."

1953 Sir Winston Leonard Spencer Churchill "for his mastery of historical and biographical description as well as for brilliant oratory in defending exalted human values."

1952 François Mauriac "for the deep spiritual insight and the artistic intensity with which he has in his novels penetrated the drama of human life."

1951 Pär Fabian Lagerkvist "for the artistic vigour and true independence of mind with which he endeavours in his poetry to find answers to the eternal questions confronting mankind."

1950 Earl (Bertrand Arthur William) Russell "in recognition of his varied and significant writings in which he champions humanitarian ideals and freedom of thought."

1949 William Faulkner "for his powerful and artistically unique contribution to the modern American novel."

1948 Thomas Stearns Eliot "for his outstanding, pioneer contribution to present-day poetry."

1947 André Paul Guillaume Gide "for his comprehensive and artistically significant writings, in which human problems and conditions have been presented with a fearless love of truth and keen psychological insight."

1946 Hermann Hesse "for his inspired writings which, while growing in boldness and penetration, exemplify the classical humanitarian ideals and high qualities of style."

1945 Gabriela Mistral "for her lyric poetry which, inspired by powerful emotions, has made her name a symbol of the idealistic aspirations of the entire Latin American world."

1944 Johannes Vilhelm Jensen "for the rare strength and fertility of his poetic imagination with which is combined an intellectual curiosity of wide scope and a bold, freshly creative style."

1943 No Nobel Prize was awarded this year

1942 No Nobel Prize was awarded this year

1941 No Nobel Prize was awarded this year

1940 No Nobel Prize was awarded this year

1939 Frans Eemil Sillanpää "for his deep understanding of his country's peasantry and the exquisite art with which he has portrayed their way of life and their relationship with Nature."

1938 Pearl Buck "for her rich and truly epic descriptions of peasant life in China and for her biographical masterpieces."

1937 Roger Martin du Gard "for the artistic power and truth with which he has depicted human conflict as well as some fundamental aspects of contemporary life in his novel-cycle Les Thibault."

1936 Eugene Gladstone O'Neill "for the power, honesty and deep-felt emotions of his dramatic works, which embody an original concept of tragedy."

1935 No Nobel Prize was awarded this year

1934 Luigi Pirandello "for his bold and ingenious revival of dramatic and scenic art."

1933 Ivan Alekseyevich Bunin "for the strict artistry with which he has carried on the classical Russian traditions in prose writing."

1932 John Galsworthy "for his distinguished art of narration which takes its highest form in *The Forsyte Saga*."

1931 Erik Axel Karlfeldt

1930 Sinclair Lewis "for his vigorous and graphic art of description and his ability to create, with wit and humour, new types of characters."

1929 Thomas Mann "principally for his great novel, *Buddenbrooks*, which has won steadily increased recognition as one of the classic works of contemporary literature."

1928 Sigrid Undset "principally for her powerful descriptions of Northern life during the Middle Ages."

1927 Henri Bergson "in recognition of his rich and vitalizing ideas and the brilliant skill with which they have been presented."

1926 Grazia Deledda "for her idealistically inspired writings which with plastic clarity picture the life on her native island and with depth and sympathy deal with human problems in general."

1925 George Bernard Shaw "for his work which is marked by both idealism and humanity, its stimulating satire often being infused with a singular poetic beauty."

1924 Wladyslaw Stanislaw Reymont "for his great national epic, *The Peasants*."

1923 William Butler Yeats "for his always inspired poetry, which in a highly artistic form gives expression to the spirit of a whole nation."

1922 Jacinto Benavente "for the happy manner in which he has continued the illustrious traditions of the Spanish drama."

1921 Anatole France "in recognition of his brilliant literary achievements, characterized as they are by a nobility of style, a profound human sympathy, grace, and a true Gallic temperament."

1920 Knut Pedersen Hamsun "for his monumental work, *Growth of the Soil*."

1919 Carl Friedrich Georg Spitteler "in special appreciation of his epic, *Olympian Spring*."

1918 No Nobel Prize was awarded this year

1917 Karl Adolph Gjellerup "for his varied and rich poetry, which is inspired by lofty ideals."

1917 Henrik Pontoppidan "for his authentic descriptions of present-day life in Denmark."

1916 Carl Gustaf Verner von Heidenstam "in recognition of his significance as the leading representative of a new era in our literature."

1915 Romain Rolland "as a tribute to the lofty idealism of his literary production and to the sympathy and love of truth with which he has described different types of human beings."

1914 No Nobel Prize was awarded this year

1913 Rabindranath Tagore "because of his profoundly sensitive, fresh and beautiful verse, by which, with consummate skill, he has made his poetic thought, expressed in his own English words, a part of the literature of the West."

1912 Gerhart Johann Robert Hauptmann "primarily in recognition of his fruitful, varied and outstanding production in the realm of dramatic art."

1911 Count Maurice (Mooris) Polidore Marie Bernhard Maeterlinck "in appreciation of his many-sided literary activities, and especially of his dramatic works, which are distinguished by a wealth of imagination and by a poetic fancy, which reveals, sometimes in the guise of a fairy tale, a deep inspiration, while in a mysterious way they appeal to the readers' own feelings and stimulate their imaginations."

1910 Paul Johann Ludwig Heyse "as a tribute to the consummate artistry, permeated with idealism, which he has demonstrated during his long productive career as a lyric poet, dramatist, novelist and writer of world-renowned short stories."

1909 Selma Ottilia Lovisa Lagerlöf "in appreciation of the lofty idealism, vivid imagination and spiritual perception that characterize her writings."

1908 Rudolf Christoph Eucken "in recognition of his earnest search for truth, his penetrating power of thought, his wide range of vision, and the warmth and strength in presentation with which in his numerous works he has vindicated and developed an idealistic philosophy of life."

1907 Rudyard Kipling "in consideration of the power of observation, originality of imagination, virility of ideas and remarkable talent for narration which characterize the creations of this world-famous author."

1906 Giosuè Carducci "not only in consideration of his deep learning and critical research, but above all as a tribute to the creative energy, freshness of style, and lyrical force which characterize his poetic masterpieces."

1905 Henryk Sienkiewicz "because of his outstanding merits as an epic writer."

1904 Frédéric Mistral "in recognition of the fresh originality and true inspiration of his poetic production, which faithfully reflects the natural scenery and native spirit of his people, and, in addition, his significant work as a Provençal philologist."

1904 José Echegaray y Eizaguirre "in recognition of the numerous and brilliant compositions which, in an individual and original manner, have revived the great traditions of the Spanish drama."

1903 Bjørnstjerne Martinus Bjørnson "as a tribute to his noble, magnificent and versatile poetry, which has always been distinguished by both the freshness of its inspiration and the rare purity of its spirit."

1902 Christian Matthias Theodor Mommsen, "the greatest living master of the art of historical writing, with special reference to his monumental work, *A History of Rome*."

1901 Sully Prudhomme "in special recognition of his poetic composition, which gives evidence of lofty idealism, artistic perfection and a rare combination of the qualities of both heart and intellect."

Dimitrios P. Naskos was born and lives in Thessaloniki, Greece. He studied musicology, cultural studies, semiotics, and creative writing. He works as a music teacher in a private school and teaches poetry and songwriting in the creative writing graduate program of the University of Western Macedonia. He writes on the Culture Books website, which specializes in poetry and organizes courses about literary theory. For many years he has written lyrics and songs, which he arranges and performs himself. He also works as a book editor.

www.ingramcontent.com/pod-product-compliance
Lightning Source LLC
LaVergne TN
LVHW042250070526
838201LV00089B/93